HERITAGE

CHARLES DICKENS IN TEESDALE

The Story of Nicholas Nickleby and the Yorkshire Schools

CHARLES DICKENS IN TEESDALE

**Written and Researched
by J. Keith Proud**

Thanks to all those people
and organisations who helped in
the preparation of this book.

Series Editor: Malcolm Parker

Published by Discovery Guides Limited,
1 Market Place, Middleton-in-Teesdale,
Teesdale, DL12 0QG. Tel: (0833) 40638

Printed by Discovery Design & Print Limited,
Cockfield, near Bishop Auckland,
Co. Durham, DL13 5BJ. Tel: (0388) 718866

ISBN O 86309 012 5 © DISCOVERY GUIDES LIMITED 1983

Preface

I wonder how many visitors to Teesdale today realise that they are following in famous footsteps.

In the first month of 1838 a young London writer came to Teesdale. His name was Charles Dickens and he came with the illustrator, Hablot Browne, to find out for himself how much truth there was in the rumours he had been hearing for many years about 'The Yorkshire Schools'. This is the true story of his visit, the people he met, the places he stayed and the villages he visited.

The man who probably suffered most as the result of Dickens' visit was William Shaw, the headmaster of Bowes Academy. As the years have passed controversy has raged as to whether he was as guilty as Dickens made out. Dickens was very careful to avoid any possibility of legal action against him by stating quite clearly in the introduction to the novel "Nicholas Nickleby" that the dreadful headmaster, Squeers, was an amalgum of many people and not a caricature of any one man. However mud sticks and Dickens threw plenty of it. The result of his researches was the novel "Nicholas Nickleby" in which the hero is sent to the village of Dotheboys, really Bowes, to work as an assistant to Mr. Squeers. A lot of the novel relating to the school is obviously set in and around Bowes.

Many of the sites are still there. You can still see Shaw's school at Dotheboys Hall in Bowes, although it has now been converted into flats. The pump which prevented Nicholas Nickleby from washing because it was frozen still stands beside the hall. You can still find warmth and refreshment in the King's Head at Barnard Castle and the Unicorn at Bowes, and in the former actually see one of the Master Humphrey's clocks. In the graveyard at Bowes you can still read some of the gravestones where boys who died while pupils at the school are buried.

Before you start to read, allow me to grant you one comforting thought; as a result of Dickens' visit to the area, the Yorkshire Schools, as an institution failed to survive for more than a couple of years.

The Maclise painting known as the 'Nickleby Portrait'.
Charles Dickens at 27 years old.

Charles Dickens at 47 years old.

Illustrations

Contents

Present day 'Dotheboys Hall' at Bowes. The old Academy of William Shaw.

8

The Background

Most people know that one of the greatest champions of social reform in the Victorian era was the writer Charles Dickens; many people are well-aware that he wrote a novel called 'Nicholas Nickleby', and almost everybody knows that Mr. Dickens visited the Barnard Castle area. This book is the story of how these three facts are linked, along with a full account of the author's stay by the banks of the River Tees. Many of the places mentioned in these pages are still there to be seen by today's visitor, some of them just as Dickens saw them.

If asked to describe Charles Dickens, most people would picture him as he was in later life, bearded and rather stern to behold, but that is an image which must be immediately discarded. When Charles Dickens came to Barnard Castle, he was only twenty-five years old, but he had been earning his living as a professional writer for several years. He had already created Mr. Pickwick and Oliver Twist, as well as a host of less well-known characters, and ahead of him lay thirty years of brilliant writing.

Charles Dickens was born on 7th February, 1812, at Landport near Portsmouth, son of a clerk in the Navy Pay Office. His father, John Dickens, was attached to the Portsmouth dockyard but the young Charles had rather an itinerant childhood. When he was two, his father was transferred to London, and then, in 1816, to Chatham in Kent. Five years later the family fell upon hard times when John Dickens lost his Navy job as a result of changes in organisation at the Admiralty.

The Dickens family had to move to London where they lodged at first in Camden Town. It was not long before John Dickens fell into debt and was imprisoned, as was the way at that time, in the Marshalsea, until his debts were settled. His family was there with him for a time, a scarring experience for them all, but particularly for the young Charles, a very sensitive boy. He was later to recall those days in 'Little Dorrit'. To avoid having to remain for too long in prison, Charles was found a job, even though it was not very savoury. At the age of ten, the little boy, and he was small for his age, was sent to work in a blacking factory at Hungerford Market. Here he was employed to label the blacking bottles, a task which he detested. He loved reading and had often been taken to the theatre in Chatham. Nothing could be further from Smollett and Fielding than this 'sweat-shop' in Hungerford. One of Dickens' characters, Mr. Micawber, is very much a reflection of his father at that time. Every night the lad had to walk four miles to his room in Camden Town, visiting his father in prison on Sundays, but he eventually found lodgings nearer.

It was not too long before John Dickens managed to obtain his release, and the family returned to Camden Town. For the next three years or so, young Charles Dickens went to school in Hampstead Road, a relatively settled period in his young life, and then he was found employment. While the boy went to work in a solicitor's office, his father also found a job as a reporter on a newspaper, 'The Morning Herald'. Charles was not happy in the law firm and decided that he, too, would try for journalism. He spent all his spare time reading, losing himself for hours in the British Museum Reading Room and also teaching himself shorthand.

When he was seventeen he achieved his ambition in that he became a reporter at Doctors' Commons, but he was, by then, flirting with the idea of becoming involved with the theatre. When he was twenty-two he became a full-time employee of a London newspaper working for 'The True Sun', and then, in 1835, for the 'Morning Chronicle'. He also wrote articles for the 'Monthly Magazine' and 'Evening Chronicle', using the nom-de-plume 'Boz'. In 1836 these papers by Dickens were published in a volume called 'Sketches by Boz' for which he was paid £150.

In 1836 the first chapters of the 'Pickwick Papers' appeared. These books were not initially printed in one volume but appeared in weekly parts in a magazine. Only later did they appear as a book. Soon after Mr. Pickwick was revealed to the public, Charles Dickens married the daughter of his friend and editor of the 'Evening Chronicle', George Hogarth. Catherine and he had ten children before their marriage ended in 1858. That was, however, many years in the future.

Dickens had been working, for Chapman and Hall, on a sporting series with the illustrator Robert Seymour, and when he died, Dickens began what was to be a long association with another artist, Hablot Browne. He worked under the name of Phiz and illustrated most of Dickens' novels.

The 'Pickwick Papers' made Dickens' reputation and he became a national celebrity. He created 'Oliver Twist' to appear in weekly instalments in 'Bentley's Miscellany', starting in 1837. It is at this point in his life that the Yorkshire journey took place. Dickens was a great observer of humanity and a superb master of the art of description, of people and their surroundings. So it was then that Dickens set off to research his next novel, 'Nicholas Nickleby'.

The Geography of the Problem

Charles Dickens had, as a boy, known hard times, and he knew the power of his pen. He had known poverty and squalor at first hand and now, as a young man with fame already opening his door, he saw all around him others trying to rise from the mire. Dickens knew that he was powerful enough to influence events to some degree and one of the institutions he wanted to put before the public was the bad boarding school. Examples of this type of establishment flourished in the far north of Yorkshire and Dickens had obviously researched the subject in some depth before or while he was contemplating his journey north.

Access to the area today is very easy in the summer with dual-carriageways facilitating travel, and tourists flock to see the beautiful countryside, but the onset of winter tells a very different story. When the snow falls it rapidly covers these high fells, and the slightest breeze whips it up from the fields and onto the roads where drifts quickly form. Further falls, which tend to be frequent at this altitude compound the situation to make the roads impassable; clearing a road, even with the sophisticated machinery in use today is a very difficult task. Imagine, then, the extent of the problem in the late 18th and early 19th century when the work of snow-clearing was done by gangs of labourers using shovels and without benefit of the telephone for the co-ordinating of such operations. At that time, villages, and even towns, could be cut off for weeks in a bad winter. As winter sets in, television viewers in the north are shown pictures of what is always the first road to be blocked by snow, the A66 just to the west of the village of Bowes. Summer visitors from the lowlands must often speculate about the black and white posts which line such high moorland roads. Their purpose is in fact to mark where the edge of the road is when the snow-ploughs come to clear the snow, and the height of these poles is some indication of the depth the snow can reach.

The schools, then, were very remote, far away from the capital where most of the pupils were recruited. Posterity has not recorded precisely how Dickens first heard of the Yorkshire schools, although he supposedly met a boy who had attended one when he himself was a boy in Chatham. This boy gave Dickens details of a grisly operation performed on him at his school, and not by a doctor. He had an abcess opened with an ordinary pen-knife. Before he came up to Yorkshire, he did some research into the subject. Today's reader may be surprised to hear that Dickens came so far to investigate the facts for himself, but, as the story unfolds, the reasons will become self-evident. It is unlikely that Dickens knew precisely how many schools there were in the Barnard Castle area, although he had probably seen advertisements for several in newspapers. It should also be stressed that they existed elsewhere in Yorkshire, and not just in the Barnard Castle region.

A lot of research has been done to ascertain the dates when these schools were in existence. Here are some as recorded in the Yorkshire Archaeology Society's edition of the records of the Parish of Bowes, in which parish many of the schools were situated. It was an extensive and sparsely populated rural area, the boys at the schools making up a large part of the population. Small villages and hamlets were linked by country roads, and Barnard Castle was the nearest market town, where much of the shopping for the schools was done. The first of the schools seems to have been set up in 1759, just as the reign of King George II was drawing to a close.

Mr. Lamb's School, Bowes	1759
Mr. Richard Jackson's School, Bowes	1764 - 1771
Mr. George Alderson Taylor's School, Bowes	1767 - 1777
Mr. Edward Johnson's School, Gilmonby	1785 - 1798
Mr. George Frederick Dote's Academy, Bowes	1788 - 1798
Mr. Thornborrow's School, Bowes	1797 - 1799
Mr. Jonathan Horn's School, Gilmonby Hall	1801 - 1822
Rev. Joseph Lambert's School, Bowes	1804 - 1806
Mr. George Chapman's School, Bowes	1804
Rev. Joseph Adamthwaite's School, Bowes	1804
Messrs. Chapman & Adamthwaite, Bowes	1808
John Adamthwaite's School, Bowes	1810 - 1816
Messrs. Shaw & Wilson's School, Bowes	1812
Mr. William Shaw's School, Bowes	1814
Mr. George Clarkson's School, Bowes	1815 - 1821
Mrs. Adamthwaite's School, Bowes	1821 - 1822
Mr. Wharton's School, Barnard Castle	1806 Closed before 1838
Messrs. Warcup & Kirkbride, Startforth House	Closed 1775
Mr. Galland's Academy, Startforth	1754
(became)	
Mr. Francis Clarke's School, Startforth	1859
Mr. Horn's School, Startforth Hall	
Mr. Edward Simpson's Academy, Woden-Croft Lodge, Barnard Castle	

An initial glance at this list suggests that there were twenty-two schools in the area, but a more considered look reveals that this was not, in fact, the case. The list spans a period of exactly one hundred years; during that century some schools closed and others opened while some establishments changed hands. As can be seen from the list, there were occasional amalgamations.

The great difficulty for the modern researcher, as for Dickens himself in his day, is to ascertain how much cruelty, and what must be termed malpractice, went on in which schools. He knew there was cruelty and he had probably heard of neglect and deaths, but, before his visit, his evidence was second and third-hand.

Before the Journey

Dickens was probably very conscious of the fact that if he presented himself as himself in front of the Yorkshire schoolmasters he would not be very successful. His name and fame had reached even to those remote fastnesses, as evidenced by a letter in the 'Durham Advertiser' newspaper of the time, about which more later. He had, therefore, to resort to subterfuge, and he laid his plans well.

Anyone venturing into alien territory needed a letter of introduction and, in Dickens' case, a 'cover story'. This he procured from a friend who came originally from Malton in Yorkshire, Charles Smithson. He was a solicitor, in practice with Dickens' schoolfriend Thomas Mitton. The firm of Smithson, Dunn and Mitton had offices at 23, Southampton Buildings, Chancery Lane, London, and they acted as Dickens' solicitors from 1838. Smithson's father had been Bailiff of Malton and the firm's other Yorkshire connection was that Charles Smithson conducted London business for a Barnard Castle lawyer, Richard Barnes. It was to this man that Dickens had an introductory letter. The letter of introduction explained that he was a gentleman seeking to explore the possibility of placing the son of a lady friend in one of the Yorkshire schools. As Dickens himself says in the preface of 'Nicholas Nickleby';

> "He (Charles Smithson) gave me some letters of introduction, in the name, I think, of my travelling companion (Browne); they bore reference to a supposititious little boy who had been left with a widowed mother who didn't know what to do with him; the poor lady had thought, as a means of thawing the tardy compassion of her relations in his behalf, of sending him to a Yorkshire school; I was the poor lady's friend, travelling that way; and if the recipient of the letter could inform me of a school in the neighbourhood, the writer would be much obliged."

The friendship of Charles Smithson was to grow over the years and Dickens was godfather to his daughter, Mary.

One fact which must be pointed out here is that although Dickens may have heard of legal cases involving the masters of the Yorkshire schools, he did not record anything of such proceedings until Friday, 2nd February 1838, the second full day of his visit to the Barnard Castle area.

It has been suggested that Dickens contemplated sending Nicholas, in the story, to a northern factory, instead of a school. However the only reference I can find among his letters to such a ploy comes almost a year after the Yorkshire visit had taken place. The letter, dated 29th December 1838 was to E.M. Fitzgerald and concerned a visit made by Dickens in November. It reads:-

> "I went some weeks ago, to Manchester, and saw the worst cotton mill. And then I saw the best. There was no great difference between them........

*But on the 11th of next month I am going down
again, only for three days, and then into the enemy's camp,
and the very head-quarters of the factory system
advocates........*

*So far as seeing goes, I have seen enough for my
purpose, and what I have seen has disgusted and astonished
me beyond all measure. I mean to strike the heaviest blow in
my power for these unfortunate creatures, but whether I
shall do so in the 'Nickleby', or wait for some other
opportunity, I have not yet determined."*

So, as he says in the 'Nickleby' preface, Dickens never forgot the
impression made on him by the boy near Rochester Castle who had
suffered under the pen-knife.

*"I was always curious about Yorkshire schools - fell, long
afterwards and at sundry times, into the way of hearing
more about them - at last, having an audience, resolved to
write about them".*

The Staging Post

Dickens was now ready to head north and as his travelling companion he had Hablot K. Browne, his illustrator, the renowned Phiz. They arrived to start their journey at the 'Saracen's Head', Snow Hill, where, in the novel, Nicholas Nickleby meets Squeers. It was at inns like this where Yorkshire schoolmasters and their young charges set off on their way north.

Nicholas has left his box at the coach-office and gone in search of Mr. Squeers.

'He found that learned gentleman sitting at breakfast, with the three little boys before noticed, and two others who had turned up by some lucky chance since the interview of the previous day, ranged in a row on the opposite seat. Mr. Squeers had before him a small measure of coffee, a plate of hot toast, and a cold round of beef; but he was at that moment intent on preparing breakfast for the little boys.

"This is twopenn'orth of milk, is it, waiter?" said Mr. Squeers, looking down into a large blue mug, and slanting it gently, so as to get an accurate view of the quantity of liquid contained in it.

"That's twopenn'orth, sir," replied the waiter.

"What a rare article milk is, to be sure, in London!" said Mr. Squeers, with a sigh, "Just fill that mug up with lukewarm water, William, will you?"

"To the wery top, sir?" inquired the waiter. "Why, the milk will be drownded."

"Never you mind that," replied Mr. Squeers. "Serve it right for being so dear. You ordered that thick bread and butter for three, did you?"

"Coming directly, sir."

"You needn't hurry yourself," said Squeers; "there's plenty of time. - Conquer your passions, boys, and don't be eager after vittles." As he uttered this moral precept, Mr. Squeers took a large bite out of the cold beef, and recognized Nicholas.

"Sit down, Mr. Nickleby," said Squeers. "Here we are, a-breakfasting, you see!"

Nicholas did not see that anybody was breakfasting except Mr. Squeers; but he bowed with all becoming reverence, and looked as cheerful as he could.

"Oh, that's the milk and water, is it, William?" said Squeers. "Very good; don't forget the bread and butter presently."

At this fresh mention of the bread and butter the five little boys looked very eager, and followed the waiter out with their eyes; meanwhile, Mr. Squeers tasted the milk and water.

"Ah!" said that gentleman, smacking his lips, "here's richness. Think of the many beggars and orphans in the streets that would be glad of this, little boys. A shocking thing hunger is, isn't it, Mr. Nickleby?"

"Very shocking, sir," said Nicholas.

"When I say number one," pursued Mr. Squeers, putting the mug before the children. "the boy on the left hand nearest the window may take a drink; and when I say number two, the boy next him will go in, and so till we come to number five, which is the last boy. Are you ready?"

"Yes, sir," cried all the little boys, with great eagerness.

"That's right," said Squeers, calmly getting on with his breakfast; "keep ready till I tell you to begin. Subdue your appetites, my dears, and you've conquered human nature. — This is the way we inculcate strength of mind, Mr. Nickleby," said the schoolmaster, turning to Nicholas, and speaking with his mouth very full of beef and toast.

Nicholas murmured something - he knew not what - in reply; and the little boys, dividing their gaze between the mug, the bread and butter (which had by this time arrived), and every morsel which Mr. Squeers took into his mouth, remained with strained eyes in torments of expectation.

"Thank God for a good breakfast," said Squeers when he had finished. "Number one may take a drink."

Number one seized the mug ravenously, and had just drunk enough to make him wish for more, when Mr. Squeers gave the signal for number two, who gave up at the same interesting moment to number three; and the process was repeated until the milk and water terminated with number five.

"And now," said the schoolmaster, dividing the bread and butter for three into as many portions as there were children, "you had better look sharp with your breakfast, for the horn will blow in a minute or two, and then every boy leaves off."

Permission being thus given to fall to, the boys began to eat voraciously, and in desperate haste; while the schoolmaster (who was in high good humour after his meal) picked his teeth with a fork, and looked smilingly on. In a very short time the horn was heard.

"I thought it wouldn't be long," said Squeers, jumping up and producing a little basket from under the seat. "Put what you haven't had time to eat in here, boys; you'll want it on the road."

Nicholas was considerably startled by these very economical arrangements.

There were two seasons when the Yorkshire schoolmasters descended on the capital, the first three weeks in January and the first three in July. They did this after having placed their advertisements in the newspapers and were in London to elicit the response and to be on

16

The Yorkshire schoolmaster at the Saracen's Head.

hand to receive new pupils. Advertisements for these schools had been appearing since 1749, and Squeers' school was advertised by Dickens in a like manner in the novel.

> *'EDUCATION, - At Mr. Wackford Squeer's Academy, Dotheboy's Hall, at the delightful village of Dotheboys, near Greta Bridge, in Yorkshire, Youth are boarded, clothed, booked, furnished with pocket money, provided with all necessaries, instructed in all languages, living and dead, mathematics, orthography, geometry, astronomy, trigonometry, the use of the globes, algebra, single stick (if required), writing, arithmetic, fortification, and every other branch of classical literature.*
>
> *Terms, twenty guineas per annum. No extras, no vacation, and diet unparalleled. Mr. Squeers is in town, and attends daily, from one till four, at the Saracen's Head, Snow Hill.'*

In this, Dickens parodied the type of advertisement with which he and his readers would be familiar. Precisely which ones Dickens had seen is not known, but there were many, of which the following are just some. Not all were still in operation when Dickens visited the area.

From the 'NORFOLK CHRONICLE' 29/4/1775
'A BOARDING SCHOOL at Stairforth, near Barnard Castle, Yorkshire: Youths are made proficient in the languages, as well as sciences, by Warcup, Kirkbride and assistants. The pupils are boarded, cloathed, and supplied with all necessaries at Twelve Pounds per year each. For character and reputation, and usage of the children, enquiry may be made of many genteel families in Norwich, whose children are now educating, several of whose parents have been at the school in person.'

There is some confusion about the last part of this advertisement since it is not made clear whether the parents mentioned had visited the school or had actually attended it as pupils themselves. The spelling in these advertisements should not be taken as an indication of lack of education on the part of the writers, presumably the masters themselves. One could, and did, spell as one wished at that time, and, since the advertisements would be hand-written to the newspapers, they could be misread. There was also the possibility of a printing error with the publisher. This probably accounts for 'Stairforth' when it should have read 'Startforth.'

Many of the advertisements were perfectly plausible;

From 'THE TIMES' 10/1/1806

'EDUCATION at BARNARD CASTLE in the COUNTY of DURHAM. At the REV. MR. WHARTON'S ACADEMY, which is placed in a very healthy situation.

YOUNG GENTLEMEN will be carefully INSTRUCTED as before the vacation, in the ENGLISH, LATIN, and GREEK LANGUAGES; in the various distinctions of WRITING, ARITHMETIC, MENSURATION, GAUGING, LAND SURVEYING, NAVIGATION, BOOK-KEEPING, &c., DRAWING, including EDUCATION and BOARD; WITH every kind of wearing apparel, and all other necessaries (Medicines and allowances excepted). THE TERMS are, if under 9 years, 16 guineas per Annum.
SATISFACTORY particulars will be given on application to MR. KIDD, No. 62, NEW BOND STREET; MR. BOWNESS, No. 7, GREEN LETTICE LANE, CANNON STREET; MR. BORRA, No. 17, WATLING STREET; MESSRS. FREARSON and SAWREY, No. 2, LAD LANE, CHEAPSIDE; or to MR. CUNNINGHAM, No. 63, POLAND STREET, SOHO, AGENT to the SCHOOL.

MR. WHARTON is in town and may be treated with for a short time from 10 to 12 in the morning every day (Sundays excepted), at the GEORGE and BLUE BOAR, HOLBORN, or at the GEORGE, ALDERMANBURY, from 3 to 4 in the evening.

MR. WHARTON has a VACANCY for 2 PARLOUR BOARDERS.'

John Galland likewise advertised the school he took over from Mr. Kirkbride, whose billing we saw earlier. He did change the wording, however;

'BOARD AND EDUCATION &c. At MR. GALLAND'S ACADEMY, STARTFORTH near BARNARD CASTLE, YORKSHIRE.

YOUNG GENTLEMEN are carefully and expeditiously taught the ENGLISH, LATIN, GREEK, FRENCH &c., LANGUAGES, WRITING, ARITHMETIC, the MATHEMATICS as far as are applicable to MERCHANTS' ACCOUNTS and LAND SURVEYING. DRAWING, NAVIGATION, GEOMETRY, GEOGRAPHY, use of the GLOBES, &c. &c., by MR. GALLAND and proper ASSISTANTS, upon moderate terms;
further particulars may be had by applying to MR. GALLAND at the BARTON COFFEE HOUSE, CHEAPSIDE, where he will attend DAILY from 11 till 2 o'clock, during his stay in town and refer applicants to people of respectability whose sons have left the SEMINARY this Christmas. N.B. - No vacations are kept except a week at this Season of the Year.
LETTERS POST PAID will be duly attended to.'

It is the 'N.B.' which makes the advertisement suspicious. What a perfect way for uncaring parents to be rid of the burden of unwanted children. They had only to be tolerated for one week in the year, and since the schools were so very far away from London, it was very much a case of 'out of sight, out of mind.'

Some of the schools even traded on their previous 'reputations';

'At Messrs. CHAPMAN and ADAMTHWAITE'S (Late Thornbarrow and Chapman) ACADEMY, BOWES, Near RICHMOND, YORKSHIRE.

Youth are carefully instructed in ENGLISH, LATIN, AND GREEK LANGUAGES, writing in various hands, ARITHMETIC, useful branches of the MATHEMATICS; ITALIAN method of book-keeping, GEOGRAPHY etc.

Strict attention is paid to their health and meals, and the greatest care is taken to protect their advancement in every branch in useful learning.

Terms including board, clothes, books and other necessaries are 17 GUINEAS a YEAR if under 9 years of age and above that age 18 GUINEAS.

Apply MR. BAINBRIDGE, No. 41 HOLBORN HILL; MR. DENT, BETHNAL GREEN; MR. HICKS, 12, WHITE-CHAPEL; MR. BLACK, 33, BISHOPSGATE WITHOUT; or to MR. HOLLAND'S COFFEE HOUSE, LOWER THAMES STREET.

MR. ADAMTHWAITE is now in TOWN and attends daily from 11 to 2 at the RAINBOW COFFEE HOUSE, CORN HILL.

The FRENCH LANGUAGE taught at a guinea extra.

All of the schools were eager to offer references;

EDUCATION
At BOWES HALL ACADEMY, near GRETA BRIDGE, YORKSHIRE.

YOUNG GENTLEMEN are plentifully Boarded and carefully instructed by MR. CLARKSON and able assistants in the ENGLISH, LATIN and GREEK LANGUAGES; Writing and Arithmetic, Book-keeping, Mensuration, and the most useful branches of Mathematics; the French language taught by a native of France.

For cards and references apply to MR. SMITH, the agent, 26, LOMBARD STREET. MR. C. will be in town in a few days, and may be treated with after his arrival at the CAROLINA COFFEE-HOUSE, BIRCHING LANE, CORNHILL.'

The most important advertisement as far as this volume is concerned is that used by William Shaw to spread abroad the 'virtues' of his school at Bowes;

EDUCATION
By MR. SHAW & ABLE ASSISTANTS
At Bowes Academy
NEAR GRETA BRIDGE, YORKSHIRE.

YOUTH are carefully instructed in the English, Latin, and Greek Languages, Writing, Common and Decimal Arithmetic; Book-keeping, Mensuration, Surveying, Geometry, Geography, and Navigation, with the most useful branches of the Mathematics, and are provided with Board, Clothes and every necessary, at TWENTY GUINEAS per

*Annum each. No extra charges whatever, Doctor's bills
excepted. No vacations, except by the Parents' desire.*

> *N.B. The French Language Two
> Guineas per Annum extra.*

> *Further Particulars may be known on application to Mr.
> W. LANKSHEAR, Surgeon, Tottenham Court, New Road;
> MRS. YOUNG, Plough Yard, Crown Street, Soho; MR.
> WALKER, 37, Drury Lane; MR. TOWNLEY, Chief Office of
> Excise, Broad Street; MR. HAMPSON, 52, Long Lane,
> Smithfield; MR. GARDINER, 80, Tottenham Court Road;
> MR. PITT, 22, Crown Court, Soho; and MR. WIGGINTON,
> 42, Museum Street, Bloomsbury.*

> *MR. SEATON, AGENT, 10, FREDERICK PLACE, Goswell
> Street Road,*

> *Will give the most respectable References to the Parents of
> others at the above Seminary, as well as to those who have
> completed their Education with MR. SHAW.*

> *ALL LETTERS MUST BE POST PAID.'*

This advertisement appeared on one of Shaw's business cards, on
the reverse of which was a list of the clothes each new boy had to take
with him to Bowes Academy;

> *'Two Suits of Clothes,
> Six Shirts,
> Six Pairs of Stockings,
> Four Night Caps,
> Four Pocket Handkerchiefs,
> Two Pairs of Shoes,
> Two Hats or One Hat and Cap.'*

Dickens and Phiz were ready to leave London to trace the route
taken by so many boys who had sallied forth into oblivion and misery.

Journey Through The Snow

Perhaps it was appropriate that Dickens' journey on Tuesday, 30th January, 1838 began at Snow Hill. The weather was not going to be good. Dickens caused Nicholas Nickleby to start his journey north from the same inn, and he paints a lively picture of the final preparations and of the journey itself;

'The little boys had to be got on top of the coach, and their boxes had to be brought out and put in, and Mr. Squeer's luggage was to be seen carefully deposited in the boot...... Nicholas mounted nimbly to his seat, and waved his hands as gallantly as if his heart went with it.

At this moment,, when the coachman and guard were comparing notes for the last time before starting on the subject of the way-bill; when porters were screwing out the last reluctant sixpences, itinerant newsmen making the last offer of a morning paper, and the horses giving a last impatient rattle to their harness, Nicholas felt somebody pulling softly at his leg. He looked down, and there stood Newman Noggs who pushed up into his hand a dirty letter....

A minute's bustle, a banging of the coach doors, a swaying of the vehicle to one side as the heavy coachman, and still heavier guard, climbed into'their seats; a cry of.........and the coach was gone too, and rattling over the stones of Smithfield.'

Remembering that the year was 1838 and that the railway system was now becoming well-established in Britain, this is one of the best and latest accounts of a way of travel which was rapidly nearing its demise;

' When the guard (who was a stout old Yorkshireman) has blown himself quite out of breath he put the horn into a little tunnel of a basket fastened to the coach-side for the purpose, and giving himself a plentiful shower of blows on the chest and shoulders, observed it was uncommon cold; after which, he demanded of every person separately whether he was going right through, and if not where he was going. Satisfactory replies being made to these queries, he surmised that the roads were pretty heavy after that fall last night, and took the liberty of asking whether any of them gentlemen carried a snuff-box. It happening that nobody did, he remarked with a mysterious air that he had heard a medical gentleman as went down to Grantham last week, say how that snuff-taking was bad for the eyes; but for his part he had never found it so, and what he said was that everybody should speak as they found. Nobody attempting to controvert this position, he took a small brown-paper parcel out of his hat, and putting on a pair of horn spectacles (the writing

Nicholas starts for Yorkshire.

being crabbed) read the direction half-a-dozen times over;
having done which he consigned the parcel to its old place,
put up his spectacles again, and stared at everybody in turn.
After this, he took another blow at the horn by way of
refreshment; and, having now exhausted his usual topics of
conversation, folded his arms as well as he could in so many
coats, and falling into a solemn silence, looked carelessly at
the familiar objects which met his eye on every side as the
coach rolled on; the only things he seemed to care for being
horses and droves of cattle, which he scrutinised with a
critical air as they were passed upon the road.

So the day wore on. At Eton Slocomb there was a good
coach dinner, of which the box, the four front outsides, the
one inside, Nicholas, the good-tempered man, and Mr.
Squeers, partook; while the five little boys were put to thaw
by the fire, and regaled with sandwiches. A stage or two
further on, the lamps were lighted.

The night and the snow came on together, and dismal
enough they were. There was no sound to be heard but the
howling of the wind; for the noise of the wheels and the tread
of the horses' feet, were rendered inaudible by the thick
coating of snow which covered the ground and was fast
increasing every moment. The streets of Stamford were
deserted as they passed through the town; and its old
churches rose, frowning and dark, from the whitened ground.
Twenty miles further on, two of the front outside passengers
wisely availing themselves of their arrival at one of the best
inns in England, turned in, for the night, at the George at
Grantham.'

The opinion that the 'George' at Grantham was one of the best inns
in England was Dickens' own. He and Phiz broke their journey there on
the way north. In his letter to his wife from Greta Bridge he writes,

'We reached Grantham between 9 and 10 on Tuesday night,
and found everything prepared for our recetpion in the very
best inn I have ever put up at. It is odd that an old lady who
had been outside all day and came in towards dinner-time
turned out to be the mistress of a Yorkshire school returning
from the holiday stay in London. She was a very queer old
lady, and showed us a long letter she was carrying to one of
the boys from his father, containing a severe lecture on his
refusing to eat boiled meat. She was very communicative,
drank a great deal of brandy and water, and towards evening
became insensible, in which state we left her.'

The first part of the journey, as far as Grantham, was probably
undertaken in a coach called the Express, which was anything but what

24

its name suggested. The next morning, Wednesday, they were up just after seven in the morning and paid just over six pounds for two places inside the Glasgow Mail, a much speedier vehicle than the Express. Dickens later recorded such a journey in 'MARTIN CHUZZLEWIT';

'The coach was none of your steady-going, yokel coaches, but a swaggering, rakish dissipated coach; up all night, and lying by all day, and leading a devil of a life. It rattled noisily through the best streets, defied the Cathedral, took the worst corners sharpest, went cutting in everywhere, making every thing get out of its way; and spun along the open country-road, blowing a lively defiance out of its key bugle, as its last glad parting legacy.

The four greys skimmed along, as if they liked it quite as well as Tom did; the bugle was in as high spirits as the greys; the coachman chimed in sometimes with his voice; the wheels hummed cheerfully in unison; the brass-work on the harness was an orchestra of little bells; and thus, as they went clinking, jingling, rattling smoothly on, the whole concern, from the buckles of the leaders' coupling-reins to the handle of the hind boot, was one great instrument of music.

Yoho, past hedges, gates, and trees; past cottages and barns, and people going home from work. Yoho, past donkey-chaises drawn aside into the ditch, and empty carts with rampant horses, whipped up at a bound upon the little water-course, and held by struggling carters close to the five-barred gate, until the coach had passed the narrow turning in the road. Yoho, by churches dropped down by themselves in quiet nooks, with rustic burial-grounds about them, where the graves are green, and daisies sleep - for it is evening - on the bosoms of the dead. Yoho, past streams, in which the cattle cool their feet, and where the rushes grow; past paddock-fences, farms, and rick-yards; past last year's stacks, cut, slice by slice, away, and showing, in the waning light, like ruined gables, old and brown. Yoho, down the pebbly dip, and through the merry water-splash, and up at a canter to the level road again. Yoho! Yoho!

Yoho, among the gathering shades; making of no account the deep reflections of the trees, but scampering on through light and darkness, Yoho, beside the village green, where cricket-players linger yet. Away with four fresh horses and the last team, with traces hanging loose, go roaming off towards the pond, until observed and shouted after by a dozen throats, while volunteering boys pursue fiery sparks, across the old stone bridge, and down again into the shadowy road, and through the open gate, and far away, away, into the wold. Yoho!

See the bright moon! High up before we know it - making the earth reflect the objects on its breast like water.

*Hedges, trees, low cottages, church steeples, blighted
stumps and flourishing young slips, have all grown vain upon
the sudden, and mean to contemplate their own fair images
till morning. The poplars yonder rustle, that their quivering
leaves may see themselves upon the ground. Not so the oak:
trembling does not become him; and he watches himself in
his stout old burly steadfastness without the motion of a
twig. The moss-grown gate, ill-poised upon its creaking
hinges, crippled and decayed, swings to and fro before its
glass, like some fantastic dowager; while our own ghostly
likeness travels on, Yoho! Yoho! through ditch and brake,
upon the ploughed land and the smooth, along the steep
hillside and steeper wall, as if it were a phantom-hunger.*

*Clouds too! And a mist upon the Hollow! Not a dull fog
that hides it, but a light, airy, gauze-like mist, which in our
eyes of modest admiration gives a new charm to the beauties
it is spread before - as real gauze has done ere now, and
would again, so please you, though we were the Pope. Yoho!
Why, now we travel like the Moon herself. Hiding this
minute in a grove of trees, next minute in a patch of vapour;
emerging now upon our broad clear course; withdrawing
now, but always dashing on, our journey is a counterpart of
hers. Yoho! A match against the Moon!'*

In the letter he was to write home to his wife, Dickens records how
the weather deteriorated after they left Grantham;

*'As we came further north, the snow grew deeper. About
eight o'clock it began to fall heavily, and as we crossed the
wild heaths hereabout, there was no vestige of a track. The
Mail kept on well, however, and at eleven we reached a bare
place with a house standing alone in the midst of a dreary
moor, which the Guard informed us was Greta Bridge. I was
in a perfect agony of apprehension, for it was fearfully cold
and there were no outward signs of anybody being up in the
house.'*

The Glasgow Mail turned west at Scotch Corner for its journey
over Stainmore, but stopped at the inns at Greta Bridge. Today's visitor
sees only the 'Morrit Arms', but there were once three hostelries here.
In the early years of the 19th century, the 'Morritt' was known as the
'George Inn' and outside was a painted sign of St. George slaying the
dragon.

The present house to the east of the bridge was then also a hostelry
and the stables, once buzzing with the activity of the ostlers can still be
seen beside the cobbled yard. This, originally was the 'Morritt Arms'

but its name was transferred to the hotel across the bridge when it ceased to be an hotel in 1845. The original 'George' was also the Post Office.

There was yet a third inn, the 'George and New Inn' which is now Thorpe Grange farm. It is half a mile to the south-east of the bridge where a road leads to Winston. This was the inn where Dickens and Browne spent the night of January 31st. As Dickens goes on to relate to his wife, the inn was not as daunting as it at first seemed;

> '....to our great joy we discovered a comfortable room with drawn curtains and a most blazing fire. In half an hour they gave us a smoking supper and a bottle of mulled port and then we retired to a couple of capital bedrooms in each of which was a rousing fire half-way up the chimney.'

The landlord at the time was George Martin who had moved here from the 'Morritt Arms' in 1826. He was also the postmaster presiding over the mail which went northwards at twenty minutes after two in the morning. Letters to the south were despatched at three in the afternoon.

It is conjectured that Dickens used the 'George and New Inn' for his hostelry in 'The Holly Tree' one of his Christmas stories, except there it is called 'The Holly Tree'. How much poetic licence was used is not known, but here are some extracts from the story concerning the inn.

> 'At nine o'clock at night, on a Yorkshire moor, a cheerful burst from our horn and a sound of talking, with a glimmering and moving about of lanterns, roused me from my drowsy state. I found that we were going to change.
>
> They helped me out, and I said to a waiter, whose bare head became as white as King Lear's in a single minute,
> "What inn is this?"
> "The Holly-Tree, sir," said he.
> "Upon my word, I believe that I must stop here," said I.
>
> Now the landlord, and landlady, and the hostler, and the post boy, and all the stable authorities, had already asked the coachman if he meant to go on. The coachman had replied, "Yes."
>
> I saw my portmanteau got out stiff, like a frozen body, then I followed the landlord, landlady, and waiter of the Holly-Tree upstairs.
>
> I thought I had never seen such a large room as that into which they showed me. It had five windows, with dark red curtains that would have absorbed the light of a general illumination; and there were complications of drapery at the top of the curtains, that went wandering about the wall in a most extraordinary manner. I asked for a smaller room and they told me there was no smaller room. They could screen

me in, however, the landlord said. They brought a great old japanned screen, with natives (Japanese, I suppose) engaged in a variety of idiotic pursuits all over it, and left me roasting whole before an immense fire.

My bedroom was some quarter of a mile off, up a great staircase at the end of a long gallery; and nobody knows what a misery this is to a bashful man who would rather not meet people on the stairs. It was the grimmest room I have ever had the nightmare in; and all the furniture, from the four posts of the bed to the two old silver candlesticks, was tall, high-shouldered, and spindle-waisted. Below, in my sitting room, if I looked round my screen, the wind rushed at me like a mad bull; if I stuck to my arm-chair, the fire scorched me to the colour of new brick. The chimney-piece was very high, and there was a bad glass - what I may call a wavy glass - above it, which, when I stood up, just showed me my anterior phrenological developments; and these never looked well, in any subject, cut short off at the eyebrow. If I stood with my back to the fire, a gloomy vault of darkness above and beyond the screen insisted on being looked at; and, in its dim remoteness, the drapery of the ten curtains of the five windows went twisting and creeping about, like a nest of gigantic worms.

When I travel, I never arrive at a place but I immediately want to go away from it. Before I had finished my supper of broiled fowl and mulled port, I had impressed upon the waiter in detail my arrangements for departure in the morning. Breakfast and bill at eight. Fly at nine. Two horses, or, if needful, even four.

Tired though I was, the night appeared about a week long.

In the morning I found that it was snowing still, that it had snowed all night, and that I was snowed up. Nothing could get out of that spot on the moor, or could come at it, until the road had been cut out by labourers. When they might cut their way to the Holly Tree, nobody could tell me.

It was now Christmas Eve. Still being snowed up was a thing I had not bargained for. I felt very lonely.'

It is strange to think that the railways were advancing at such a rate that, two years after Dickens' visit to the inn at Greta Bridge, there were very few coaches still operating in the land and two of the three Greta Bridge inns had to close through the resultant lack of custom.

Barnard Castle

Before Dickens left the 'George and New Inn' at Greta Bridge he wrote to his wife at 48, Doughty Street, London. It was Thursday February 1st. The letter has been quoted earlier, and it continues;

> *'We have had for breakfast, toasts, cakes, a yorkshire pie, a piece of beef about the size and much the shape of my portmanteau, tea, coffee, ham and eggs - and are now going to to look about us. Having finished our discoveries we start in a postchaise for Barnard Castle which is only four miles off, and there I deliver the letter given me by Mitton's friend. All the schools are round about that place, and a dozen old abbies besides, which we shall visit by some means or other tomorrow. We shall reach York on Saturday I hope, and (God willing) I trust I shall be at home on Wednesday Morning. If anything should occur to prevent me, I will write to you from York, but I think that is not likely.'*

Dickens, then, left Greta Bridge in a post-chaise and travelled through the snow-covered countryside to the market town of Barnard Castle. It lay four miles away, and on their arrival, the two friends went to the 'King's Head' where they took rooms. The hotel is still there, although its appearance externally and internally has changed since 1838. It stands just up the bank from the old Market Cross. We do not know for certain which rooms our travellers occupied but Dickens had a bedroom and a sitting room in what is now the old part of the hotel. From the sitting room he probably used, Dickens would have had a good view if the market place and the shops on the far side of it.

The family who ran the hotel during Dickens' stay had acquired it very early in the 19th century. Richard Harrison took it over from Robert Wood. On Harrison's death, the management was taken over by Ann and Jane, his two daughters who took up the proprietorship in 1826. In 1830, on December 2nd in fact, Jane Harrison married one Henry Ewbank who was the landlord when Dickens arrived. The inn stayed in the family until 1906.

Dickens presented his letter of introduction in Barnard Castle, having had, until then, no reason to use it. He showed it when he called at the office of a solicitor called Barnes, in Galgate. This is how Dickens describes the incident in the preface to 'Nicholas Nickleby';

> *'I went to several places in that part of the country where I understood the schools to be most plentifully sprinkled, and had no occasion to deliver a letter until I came to a certain town which shall be nameless. The person to whom it was addressed, was not at home; but he came down at night, through the snow, to the inn where I was staying. It was after dinner; and he needed little persuasion to sit down by the fire in a warm corner, and take his share of the wine that was on the table.*

An old photograph of Barnard Castle (c.1870) from outside the King's Head Hotel

I am afraid he is dead now. I recollect he was a jovial, ruddy, broad-faced man; that we got acquainted directly; and that we talked on all kinds of subjects, except the school, which he showed a great anxiety to avoid. "Was there any large school near?" I asked him, in reference to the letter. "Oh yes," he said; "there was a pratty big 'un." "Was it a good one?" I asked. "Ey!" he said, "it was as good as anoother; that was a' a matther of opinion;" and fell to looking at the fire, staring round the room, and whistling a little. On my reverting to some other topic that we had been discussing, he recovered immediately; but, though I tried him again and again, I never approached the question of the school, even if he were in the middle of a laugh, without observing that his countenance fell, and that he became uncomfortable. At last, when we had passed a couple of hours or so, very agreeably, he suddenly took up his hat, and leaning over the table and looking me full in the face, said, in a low voice: "Weel Misther, we've been vara pleasant toogather, and ar'll spak' my moind tiv'ee. Dinnot let the weedur send her lattle boy to yan o' our school-measthers, while there's a harse to hoold in a' Lunnon, or a gootther to lie asleep in. Ar wouldn't mak' ill words amang my neeburs, and ar speak tiv'ee quiet loike. But I'm dom'd if ar can gang to bed and not tellee, for weedur's sak', to keep the lattle boy from a' sike scoondrels while there's a harse to hoold in a' Lunnun, or a gootther to lie asleep in!" Repeating these words with great heartiness, and with a solemnity on his jolly face that made it look twice as large as before, he shook hands and went away. I never saw him afterwards.'

In a letter written to Mrs. S.C. Hall on December 29th 1838, almost a year after the event, Dickens contradicts the statement in the preface by telling how he met the solicitor on two occasions. He refers to him in the letter as 'the man of business';

'The man of business gave an introduction to one or two schools, but at night he came down to the Inn where I was stopping, and after much hesitation and confusion - he was a large-headed flat-nosed red-faced old fellow - said with a degree of feeling one would not have given him credit for, that the matter had been upon his mind all day - that they were sad places for mothers to send their orphan boys too - that he hoped I would not give him up as my adviser - but that she had better do anything with them - let them hold horses, run-errands - fling them in any way upon the mercy of the World - rather than trust them there. This was an attorney, a well-fed man of business, and a rough Yorkshireman!'

The interesting fact about the meeting with the solicitor, 'the red-faced old fellow' is that Richard Barnes, the solicitor who was practising in 1838, was only 31 years old. Was it then his relation, John Barnes whom Dickens met! He had been in practice in the town since at least 1822 and had been joined by Richard in 1829, but by 1832 John had retired. Strangely enough Richard ceased to practise in the town in 1847. In the 1848 preface to the novel, Dickens tells his readers that 'I am afraid he is dead now!' This could well have been a ploy to deter anyone from hunting out the fellow.

The solicitor was supposedly the prototype of John Browdie whom Nicholas first meets at a tea-party presided over by Miss Squeers who introduces the two men;

> '"I beg your pardon," interposed Miss Squeers, hastening to do the honours, "Mr. Nickelby - Mr. John Browdie."
>
> "Servant, sir," said John, who was something over six feet high, with a face and body rather above the due proportion than below it.
>
> "Yours to command, sir," replied Nicholas, making fearful ravages on the bread and butter.
>
> Mr. Browdie was not a gentleman of great conversational powers, so he grinned twice more, and having now bestowed his customary mark of recognition on every person in the company, grinned at nothing in particular and helped himself to food.
>
> "Old wooman awa', bean't she? said Mr. Browdie, with his mouth full.
>
> Miss Squeers nodded assent.
>
> Mr. Browdie gave a grin of special width, as if he thought that really was something to laugh at, and went to work at the bread and butter with increased vigour. It was quite a sight to behold how he and Nicholas emptied the plate between them.
>
> "Ye wean't get bread and butther ev'ry neight, I expect, mun," said Mr. Browdie, after he had sat staring at Nicholas a long time over the empty plate.
>
> Nicholas bit his lip, and coloured, but affected not to hear the remark.
>
> "Ecod," said Mr. Browdie, laughing boisterously, "they dean't put too much intiv'em. Ye'll be nowt but skeen and boans if you stop here long eneaf.
>
> Ho! ho! ho!"

Brodie is encountered later in the story as Nicholas is on the road from Dotheboys Hall to Greta Bridge having thrashed Squeers;

> 'He beheld a horseman coming towards him, whom on nearer approach he discovered, to his infinite chagrin, to be

no other than Mr. John Browdie, who, clad in cords and leather leggings, was urging his animal forward by means of a thick ash stick which seemed to have been recently cut from some stout sapling.

"I am in no mood for more noise and riot," thought Nicholas, "and yet, do what I will, I shall have an altercation with this honest blockhead, and perhaps a blow or two from yondr staff."

In truth, there appeared some reason to expect that such a result would follow from the encounter; for John Browdie no sooner saw Nicholas advancing than he reined in his horse by the footpath, waited until such time as he should come up - looking, meanwhile, very sternly between the horse's ears at Nicholas as he came on at his leisure.

"Servant, young genelman," said John.

"Yours," said Nicholas.

"Weel, we ha' met at last," observed John, making the stirrup ring under a smart touch of the ash stick.

"Yes," replied Nicholas hesitating. "Come!" he said frankly, after a moment's pause; "we parted on no very good terms the last time we met. It was my fault, I believe; but I had no intention of offending you, and no idea that I was doing so. I was very sorry for it afterwards. Will you shake hands?"

"Shake honds!" cried the good-humoured Yorkshireman; "ah! that I weel." At the same time he bent down from the saddle, and gave Nicholas's fist a huge wrench. "But wa'at be the matther wi' thy feace, mun? it be all brokken loike."

"It is a cut," said Nicholas, turning scarlet as he spoke - "a blow; but I returned it to the giver, and with good interest too."

"Noa, did'ee, though?" exclaimed John Browdie. "Well deane! I loike 'un for thot."

"The fact is," said Nicholas, not very well knowing how to make the avowal - "the fact is that I have been ill-treated."

"Noa," interposed John Browdie, in a tone of compassion - for he was a giant in strength and stature, and Nicholas very likely in his eyes seemed a mere dwarf - "dean't say thot."

"Yes, I have," replied Nicholas - "by that man Squeers; and I have beaten him soundly, and am leaving this place in consequence."

"What!" cried John Browdie, with such an ecstatic shout that the horse quite shied at it - "beatten the school-measther! Ho! ho! ho! Beatten the schoolmeaster! who ever heard o' the loike o' that noo! Giv' us thee hond agean, yoongster. Beatten the schoolmeasther! Dang it, I loove thee for't!"

With these expressions of delight John Browdie laughed

Nicholas astonishes Mr. Squeers and family.

and laughed again - so loud that the echoes far and wide sent back nothing but jovial peals of merriment - and shook Nicholas by the hand, meanwhile, no less heartily. When his mirth had subsided, he enquired what Nicholas meant to do; on his informing him to go straight to London, he shook his head doubtfully, and inquired if he knew how much the coaches charged to carry passengers so far.

"No, I do not," said Nicholas; "but it is of no great consequence to me, for I intend walking."

"Gang awa' to Lunnun afoot!" cried John, in amazement.

"Every step of the way," replied Nicholas. "I should be many steps further on by this time, and so good-bye!"

"Nay, noo," replied the honest countryman, reining in his impatient horse, "stan' still, tell'ee. Hoo much cash hast thee gotten?"

"Not much," said Nicholas, colouring, "but I can make it enough. Where there's a will there's a way, you know."

John Browdie made no verbal answer to this remark, but putting his hand in his pocket pulled out an old purse of soiled leather, and insisted that Nicholas should borrow from him whatever he required for his present necessities.

"Dean't be afeard, mun," he said; "tak' eneaf to carry thee whoam. Thee'lt pay me yan day, a' warrant."

Nicholas could by no means be prevailed upon to borrow more than a sovereign, with which loan Mr. Browdie, after many entreaties that he would accept of more (observing, with a touch of Yorkshire caution, that if he didn't spend it all he could put the surplus by till he had an opportunity of remitting it carriage free), was fain to content himself.

"Tak' that bit o' timber to help thee on wi', mun," he added, pressing his stick on Nicholas, and giving his hand another squeeze; "keep a good heart and bless thee. Beatten the schoolmeasther! 'God it's the best thing a've heerd this twonty year!'

In between his first visit to Barnes and the meeting in the 'King's Head' that evening, Dickens was not idle. He went to a school run by a Mr. McKay who had formerly been an usher at William Shaw's school. McKay's school was on the top floor of a building near the bottom of the part of town known as the Bank. It was McKay who related to Dickens an account of life at Shaw's school, but it is recorded that McKay had not got on well with Shaw and probably seized the opportunity to have revenge on the man who had dismissed him. There can be little doubt that it was McKay who gave Dickens the information which caused him to enter in his diary the next day;

('Mem. Shaw the schoolmaster we saw to-day, is the man in whose school several boys went blind sometime since, from

gross neglect. The case was tried, and the verdict went against him. It must have been between 1823 and 1826. Look this out in the Newspapers.)'

Although Richard Barnes ceased to practise in 1847, he did not die until 1861. He lies buried in Barnard Castle. Why then did he cease his profession at the age of only forty?

On his first day in the market town, Dickens had a good look round the place and it was then, at Amen Corner, that he saw the clock shop owned by a clockmaker called Thomas Humphrey. Dickens talked to him and to his son William. It was William who made the 'centre-second pendulum clock, dead-beat movement, possessing a compensation pendulum for change of temperature.' It was this clock which supposedly attracted Dickens' attention to the shop, although it has been suggested that the clock was always kept well inside the shop and Dickens could not have seen it from the street. As well as clocks, the subject of schools was raised, and, apparently, Thomas Humphrey suggested that Dickens should visit William Shaw's school at Bowes. There is one school of thought which believes that Thomas Humphrey, then aged fifty-one, went to Shaw's school with Dickens the next day to act as his guide, but there is no evidence to support this theory so far as can be traced.

Charles Dickens used Thomas Humphrey's clock as the basis for his book, 'Master Humphrey's Clock', and there can be no doubt that the gentleman's business prospered as a result of the publicity he received from the eminent author. When Dickens visited the shop it was beside the church, but four years later, in 1842, Humphrey moved to more extensive premises at 9, Market Place, opposite the 'King's Head'. Richard Barnes, the solicitor, rented part of the premises from Master Humphrey. His offices were above and behind the clockmaker's.

William Humphrey moved to Hartlepool soon after Dickens' visit and started his own business, taking with him the original clock immortalised by the author. Thomas replaced it with a large round-faced clock bearing his name which he placed over the door of his new shop. Thomas had a second son, Thomas Gibson Humphrey, who joined his father is business. When he died in 1857, aged only thirty-six, old Thomas took down the clock and sent it to William at Middlegate in Hartlepool, but the old man erected another timepiece in the same place before the year was out. Old Thomas died in 1868 and the third clock was sold in Newcastle, the buyer thinking that it was the original 'Master Humphrey's Clock', since it had with it a letter from Dickens himself to Thomas Humphrey.

If you wish to see one of Thomas Humphrey's clocks today, there is one at the top of the staircase in the'King's Head', but it is a relatively recent acquisition and was not there in 1838.

By the end of Thursday, Dickens had talked to many people, not all of them recorded, and was ready to journey south of the Tees, across the county border from Durham into Yorkshire.

The Yorkshire Schools

Charles Dickens and Hablot K. Browne left the 'King's Head' on the morning of Friday, February 2nd. The weather was still wintry. We do not know the route they took but their eventual destination was Bowes, a small village up on the moors to the south of Barnard Castle. A picture of the day spent by the two travellers can be pieced together. He says in the 'Nickleby' preface that he went to

> 'several places in that part of the country where I understand the schools to be most plentifully sprinkled.'

We know that the boys who attended the schools were, in many cases, unwanted children who could be boarded at these establishments for years without any holidays at all. Their parents or guardians had no need to visit them if they did not wish to do so, as long as the bills were paid. None of the teachers in their advertisements were keen to disclose their qualifications to be runnning a school, but they had no legal need of any, since there were no statutory rules governing the setting up and running of schools at that time. There was, however, need for some capital to purchase or lease some property. In the original preface to 'Nicholas Nickleby' Dickens talks about the Yorkshire schools where there were

> 'lasting agonies and disfigurements inflicted upon children by the treatment of the masters in those places....neglect, cruelty and disease as no writer of fiction would have the boldness to imagine.'

Dickens and Browne had lunch at the 'Unicorn' in Bowes so, unless they left Barnard Castle very late that morning, they probably travelled via Startforth just over the River from Barnard Castle. This can be deduced because the ride to Bowes by chaise would take no longer than half an hour to an hour, assuming that there were not too many delays caused by the snow.

Startforth, up a steep bank from the Tees, had at least two and possibly three of the schools which Dickens sought, and he had made enquiries about the schools there.

An account survives of life at Startforth Hall, a school which had formerly been at Bowes. The boy was at the school, which he calls Stratford Hall, when its location was changed;

> '"The school was close to Barnard Castle, but was first at Bowes. Bowes is some five miles from the castle. I went to the school in 1805 or 1806. Mr. Horn was the master. He had three assistants, Robinson, Hardy, and a hunchbacked man - the latter a spiteful old fellow, who used to take much pleasure in punishing the boys. I was a parlour-boarder. The board was rather poor. For breakfast we had oatmeal porridge with 'treacle'. Dinner consisted generally of pork and mashed potatoes. On wash-days the latter meal was changed to bread and milk, the quantity ad lib. The supper generally was brown bread and milk. I was at the school

A C19th photograph of the 'Unicorn' at Bowes.

*about two years and a half. After I had been at the school two
years, it was removed to Barnard Castle. The teacher and
assistants remained unchanged. The new school was at
Stratford Hall, a fine old country place, a farm house, and the
teacher rented some land with it, and kept some twenty
cows. Many of the scholars used to help in haymaking, for
which they got an extra pat of butter for their tea. The school
had forty or fifty scholars, twenty of the number being
parlour-boarders. There was some favour shown these
parlour-boarders, above the other scholars. Sometimes they
got a pudding which the others did not participate in. In the
spring the boys had to take a dose of salts all round, and two
or theree times in the summer a spoonful of sulphur and
molasses."'*

The 'Unicorn' at Bowes was a coaching inn, but it survived after the
demise of the vehicle which brought it so much business.

So many stories surround Dickens' visit to the area that it really is
difficult to sort fact from fiction. There is absolutely no doubt that
Dickens met Shaw but how long the interview lasted is not known. He
also had time to visit the church. Whether he spent the night at the
'Unicorn' or returned to Barnard Castle and the 'King's Head' is also
open to conjecture as the fact is not recorded.

Local tradition says that Dickens did go into Shaw's Academy at
Dotheboy's Hall but that Shaw, having been warned of his imminent
arrival, showed him very briefly round the establishment before
sending him away.

Did Dickens visit any of the other schools in the village, and did
Shaw know that his visitor was the famous author? One cannot help but
feel that in both cases the answer must have been in the affirmative.
Surely, even in this remote part of Britain, the presence of such a
famous personage as Charles Dickens could not long go undetected. He
reputedly used his own name when he lodged at the 'King's Head'. He
was in the area only two full days, however, as he left for Darlington and
the south on Saturday morning. Visitors to the region will still,
however, be told that he was here for at least a month. This belief may
have grown in part from the memoirs of H.F. Lloyd, a former pupil at
Bowes Academy. His reminiscences were published in the 'Glasgow
Evening Times' in 1866, and I will refer to them again later. This extract
is about a return visit made by H.F. Lloyd to the north-east of England
while engaged in his professional acting career;

*'A few years ago, when passing through Barnard Castle
(which is just three miles from Bowes), I myself heard that
Dickens had resided there for some time. The same barber
that shaved me had attended him often.*

*He (the barber) pointed out to me a little inn close by as
the house in which Dickens lodged, and added that he used to
walk over to Bowes two or three times a week, that he was*

known to be always writing, and that no one could make out
who or what he was. After the novel appeared, however, its
author was put down by all the people thereabouts as the
man who used to write so much, and inquire so particularly
about Bowes. But further. In the year 1871 my son Arthur,
myself, and one or two others, made a short professional tour
in England. Amongst the towns we visited was Sunderland.
We put up there at the Palatine Hotel, then kept by a Mr.
Thompson, and remained for a week. At night, after our
entertainment was over, we used to sit in the bar parlour,
and there one evening we met an old lady of the name of
Ewebank, an aunt of Mrs. Thompson. In the course of
conversation she informed me that she came from Yorkshire,
from Barnard Castle. I felt rather interested at this, and
asked her if she had known a Mr. Shaw of Bowes.
"Intimately," she replied, "for years." I then inquired if she
had ever seen Dickens, the author of "Nicholas Nickleby."
"See him" she answered, "why he lived with us at Barnard
Castle for months; my husband kept the King's Head, where
he stayed." This was the very little inn that, as I have
mentioned, was pointed out to me by the barber, and so I got
more anxious to hear all I could from the old lady.
Accordingly, I next asked - "Did you know John Browdie?"
"Quite well," she said; "his real name was John F....., of
Broadiswood, a farmer, and he married a Miss Dent, a cousin
of Miss Shaw's." In continuing, Mrs. Ewebank told me that
Dickens walked two or three times a week to Bowes to see
Mr. Shaw, and often spent the day there; that he was always
writing, and was supposed by them to be a commercial
traveller. On her asking him once if he had known Mr. Shaw
long, he replied, "Since I was a boy; but I haven't seen him
for some time until lately. I lived in the neighbourhood then."
After he left the King's Head, she never saw or heard of him
again; but, when the novel came out, they all said - "that
must be the man who was always here, and was so often at
Mr. Shaw's."'

One can see how the real facts of the visit had become exaggerated
even by 1886. The old lady called here 'Ewebank' must have been Henry
Ewbank's wife, the former Jane Harrison, and surely every tradesman
in Barnard Castle must have claimed, like the barber, to have had
dealings with Dickens. Mrs. Ewebank's remark about her reaction after
the appearance of the novel leads one to think that she did not know
Dickens by his real name at the 'King's Head', but then the rest of her
account is such an obvious tissue of fabrications that little regard can be
paid to her testimony.

Mrs. Ewbank was even totally wrong with her facts about the man
who married Miss Dent, Miss Shaw's cousin. The lady's name was Mary

Dent and she actually married one Thomas Todd, a gentleman and farmer of Stanhope in Weardale on 10th May, 1832. There were three witnesses at the wedding in Bowes church. One was William Shaw, another was his daughter, Mary Ann Shaw, and the third was one of his wife's relatives, John Laidman.

Equally unlikely is another part of Lloyd's memoirs. This time he is writing about a letter he received from another old boy of Bowes Academy who also seems to have his facts more than a little confused;

> '"By the by, how strange that none of Charles Dickens's friends ever mentioned that he was at Dotheboys Hall. I see no disgrace in it, indeed, I think there is much credit due to our old usher Mackay that many of his pupils have turned out so well in life. In fact, I'm thinking of writing to the Telegraph, stating that Dickens received the best part of his education at Shaw's desk, who used to act in our private theatricals, a great favourite of Shaw's, who never passed him without saying a word of encouragement to him? This was Dickens. Shaw little thought that the boy he was so praising would be his ruin in after life, &c., &c., - Yours sincerely, M.S."'

Dickens claims that the Squeers in the novel is not an actual person but a composite of several schoolmasters whom he met.

The preface of Nicholas Nickleby again;

> 'Of the monstrous neglect of education in England, and the disregard of it by the State as a means of forming good or bad citizens, and miserable or happy men, private schools long afforded a notable example. Although any man who had proved his unfitness for any other occupation in life, was free, without examination or qualification, to open a school anywhere; although preparation for the functions he undertook, was required in the surgeon who assisted to bring a boy into the world, or might one day assist, perhaps, to send him out of it; in the chemist, the attorney, the butcher, the baker, the candlestick maker; the whole round of crafts and trades, the schoolmaster excepted; and although schoolmasters, as a race, were the blockheads and imposters who might naturally be expected to spring from such a state of things, and to flourish in it; these Yorkshire schoolmasters were the lowest and most rotten round in the whole ladder. Traders in the avarice, indifference, or imbecility of parents, and the helplessness of children; ignorant, sordid, brutal men, to whom few considerate persons would have entrusted the board and lodging of a horse or a dog; they formed the worthy cornerstone of a structure, which for absurdity and a magnificent high-minded laissez-aller neglect, has rarely been exceeded in the world.

41

We hear sometimes of an action for damages against the unqualified medical practitioner, who has deformed a broken limb in pretending to heal it. But, what of the hundreds of thousands of minds that have been deformed for ever by the incapable pettifoggers who have pretended to form them!'

In his letter to Mrs. S.C. Hall, Dickens writes that William Shaw was a 'scoundrel' and goes on:-

'....if I am not much mistaken an action was brought against him by the parents of a miserable child, a cancer in whose head he' (Shaw) 'opened up with an inky penknife and so caused his death.'

Here it is Dickens who has his facts wrong. He is mixing up Shaw with the headmaster of the boy he had met as a child. Actually, both stories were untrue, or so it seems, because the 'Newcastle Weekly Chronicle' of 1886 came up with an account by the boy who told Dickens the tale. On Christmas Eve that year, the paper reported that the boy had been a pupil at Clarkson's school and that he had used the penknife on himself to remove a pimple from his own nose. At last then we have incontrovertible proof that Dickens ascribed to Shaw an incident with which he had no connection. He even has Mrs. Squeers performing the operation, in Chapter 34 of 'Nicholas Nickleby.'

Dickens, nevertheless, claims that Wackford Squeers is not based on Shaw and this is his famous account of Squeers;

'Mr. Squeers' appearance was not prepossessing. He had but one eye, and the popular prejudice runs in favour of two. The eye he had was unquestionably useful, but decidedly not ornamental, being of a greenish-grey, and in shape resembling the fanlight of a street door. The blank side of his face was much wrinkled and puckered up, which gave him a very sinister appearance, especially when he smiled, at which times his expression bordered closely on the villainous. His hair was very flat and shiny, save at the ends, where it was brushed stiffly up from a low protruding forehead, which assorted well with his harsh voice and course manner. He was about two or three and fifty, and a trifle below the middle size; he wore a white neckerchief with long ends, and

a suit of scholastic black; but his coat sleeves being a great deal too long and his trousers a great deal too short, he appeared ill at ease in his clothes, and as if he were in a perpetual state of astonishment at finding himself so respectable.'

For an eye-witness description of William Shaw we must return to H.F. Lloyd, the actor, and his account of his days as a pupil at Bowes Academy;

'But what I consider the most interesting period of my school-days has now to be referred to. It was the twelve months, or thereabouts, which, after leaving Pike's, I spent at Bowes Academy, by Greta Bridge, Durham, immortalised in "Nicholas Nickleby" as "Dotheboys' Hall," Yorkshire, and the headmaster of which was a most worthy and kind-hearted, if somewhat peculiar, gentleman named William Shaw, whom Dickens, to suit his own purposes, chose to pillory as Mr. Squeers. I can see him now as plainly as I did then, and can testify to the truth of the outward presentment of the man as described by Dickens, and depicted by his artist in the pages of the novel allowing, of course, for both being greatly exaggerated. A sharp, thin, upright little man, with a slight scale covering the pupil of one of the eyes. Yes. There he stands, with his Wellington boots and short black trousers, not originally cut too short, but from a habit he had of sitting with one knee over the other, and the trousers being tight, they would get "ruck'd" half-way up the boots. Then, the clean white vest, swallow-tailed black coat, white neck-tie, silver-mounted spectacles, close cut iron-grey hair, high-crowned hat worn slightly at the back of his head - and there you have the man.

But what was the school itself like? and how about the poor Smikes? - it may be asked. Well, I can answer as to that, and maintain the truth of every word I write. It was a fine large establishment, with every accommodation required. It was in a lovely situation, surrounded by a beautiful garden, the beck running past at the foot of the hill, and the romantic ruin of Bowes Castle within a hundred yards of the house, just outside the garden wall. The interior of the house was kept scrupulously clean, twelve female servants at least being employed. The food was excellent, and as much as you could eat; the boys well clad - shoemakers and tailors on the premises - for be it known that the boys were clothed, as well as boarded and educated, and all, if my memory be correct, for some £20 a year. No such a thing as a Smike was to be seen here, and there was less punishment for inattention than in any other school I ever attended. "Save in the way of kindness," I never, except once, knew Mr. Shaw to lift his hand to a boy the whole time I was there. He would walk round the schoolroom, look over us while writing, and here and there pat a boy on the head, saying, "Good boy - good boy; you'll be a great man some day, if you pay attention to your lessons. If a lad was ill, he would sit by his bed-side and play the flute - on which he was an adept - for an hour or two together to amuse him. And this was the man whom Dickens transformed into the illiterate tyrannical, brutal pedagogue Squeers!'

How far can we believe Lloyd? Surely we must give him as much credence as we give Dickens. Incidentally T.P. Cooper maintains that Dickens and Browne did not gain entry to Shaw's school. Shaw had heard that they were coming and so doubted their credentials when they appeared on his doorstep. He 'received them coldly' and refused to show them round the school, an act which made Dickens even more suspicious, but he had at least met the man. Lloyd was after all a pupil of Shaw's or so he says.

Here in comparison, then, is Dickens' portrait of Squeers pupils:-

It was such a crowded scene, and there were so many objects to attract attention, that at first Nicholas stared about him, really without seeing anything at all. By degrees, however, the place resolved itself into a bare and dirty room, with a couple of windows, whereof a tenth part might be of glass, the remainder being stopped up with old copy-books and paper. There were a couple of long, old, rickety desks, cut and notched, and inked, and damaged in every possible way; two or three forms; a detached desk for Squeers, and another for his assistant. The ceiling was supported, like that of a barn, by cross beams and rafters; and the walls were so stained and discoloured that it was impossible to tell whether they had ever been touched with paint or whitewash.

But the pupils - the young noblemen! How the last faint traces of hope, the remotest glimmering of any good to be derived from his efforts in this den, faded from the mind of Nicholas as he looked in dismay around! Pale and haggard faces, lank and bony figures, children with the countenances of old men, deformities with irons upon their limbs, boys of stunted growth, and others whose long, meagre legs would hardly bear their stooping bodies, all crowded on the view together; there were the bleared eye, the hare lip, the

The internal economy of Dotheboys Hall.

*crooked foot, and every ugliness or distortion that told of
unnatural aversion conceived by parents for their offspring,
or of young lives which, from the earliest dawn of infancy,
had been one horrible endurance of cruelty and neglect.
There were little faces which should have been handsome,
darkened with the scowl of sullen, dogged suffering; there
was childhood with the light of its eye quenched, its beauty
gone, and its helplessness alone remaining; there were
vicious-faced boys, brooding with leaden eyes, like
malefactors in a jail; and there were young creatures on
whom the sins of their frail parents had descended, weeping
even for the mercenary nurses they had known, and
lonesome even in their loneliness. With every kindly
sympathy and affection blasted in its birth, with every young
and healthy feeling flogged and starved down, with every
revengeful passion that can fester in swollen hearts eating
its evil way to their core in silence, what an incipient Hell
was breeding here!*

*And yet this scene, painful as it was, had its grotesque
features, which in a less interested observer than Nicholas
might have provoked a smile. Mrs. Squeers stood at one of
the desks, presiding over an immense basin of brimstone and
treacle, of which delicious compound she administered a
large instalment to each boy in succession, using for the
purpose a common wooden spoon, which might have been
originally manufactured for some gigantic top, and which
widened every young gentleman's mouth considerably - they
being all obliged, under heavy corporal penalties, to take in
the whole of the bowl at a gasp. In another corner, huddled
together for companionship, were the little boys who had
arrived on the preceding night, three of them in very large
leather breeches, and two in old trousers, a something
tighter fit than drawers are usually worn; at no great
distance from these was seated the juvenile son and heir of
Mr. Squeers - a striking likeness of his father - kicking with
great vigour, under the hands of Smike, who was fitting upon
him a pair of new boots that bore a most suspicious
resemblance to those which the least of the little boys had
worn on the journey down - as the little boy himself seemed
to think, for he was regarding the appropriation with a look
of most rueful amazement.*

*Besides these, there was a long row of boys waiting,
with countenances of no pleasant anticipation, to be treacled;
and another file, who had just escaped from the infliction,
making a variety of wry mouths, indicative of any but
satisfaction. The whole were attired in such motley, ill-
assorted, extra-ordinary garments as would have been
irresistibly ridiculous, but for the foul appearance of dirt,
disorder, and disease with which they were associated.'*

Had Dickens witnessed such a scene? One can hardly believe that, should such an array of misery have been in evidence at Bowes Academy, Shaw would have allowed Dickens to witness it; and yet, even given Dickens' great literary powers, there is more than a little which rings so true;

> 'He could not but observe how silent and sad the boys all seemed to be. There was none of the noise and clamour of a schoolroom, none of its boisterous play or hearty mirth. The children sat crouching and shivering together, and seemed to lack the spirit to move about. The only pupil who evinced the slightest tendency towards locomotion or playfulness was Master Squeers, and as his chief amusement was to tread upon the other boys' toes in his new boots, his flow of spirits was rather disagreeable than otherwise.'

Before we become too convinced that this kind of school was nothing more than a figment of Dickens' fertile imagination, here is an account of some time spent by a boy at a school in Cotherstone, not very far from Bowes, but in no way related to Dickens' visit. This tale does at least have a happy ending. The account was related by the author in 1834, three years before Dickens' visit to the region and has not been influenced by the publicity given to the schools after that event. The name of the boy was James Abernethy and he was at the school in 1827. The master of Cotherstone School was a man by the name of Smith;

> "My father had long been speaking of putting me and brothers to a boarding school, and being taken with Mr. Smith's advertisement in a newspaper in which he described himself as 'a benevolent teacher of youth, called upon him at the Belle Sauvage Inn, Ludgate Hill, whither he used to repair periodically, for the purpose of securing new pupils, and was then staying on one of these ventures. Not finding him at home he left his card, and on the following day this worthy gentleman entered our house, demonstrated or at least attempted to demonstrate with great warmth the excellency of his system, called his scholars 'his dear children,' and, in fact, so won the respect of my unsuspecting parents that my father thought him a happy man, and my mother regarded him as a saint. I was to learn 'good breeding' and he engaged to teach me the classics, mathematics, etc., with board and lodging also, all for the moderate sum of £20 per annum. How well he fulfilled his promise will be hereafter shown, suffice it to say that parents cannot be too careful of sending their sons to be adepts at all kinds of roguery and mischief, and are anxious to see them exalted in this peculiar manner above their fellow men, why then, by all means, send them to one of the cheap Yorkshire boarding schools.
>
> "However, to this fellow's care my brother George and myself were entrusted, and we made our voyage with him in

47

a brig bound to Stockton-on-Tees, which occupied several days, our fellow passengers, being a cockney girl who was going to Stockton for her health, the captain's wife and children, a monkey, who was a venerable patriarch, and a pig. Mrs. Smith, tender hearted creature! had driven all the way from the academy (or prison) a distance of thirty-six miles, to meet her beloved husband, and was waiting for us at the inn on arrival, but being, as I said before, a tender-hearted creature, and being moreover afraid that the joy of meeting her husband might prove too much for her weak nerves, she had fortified her courage with a good bolus of brandy, so that when we met her she was in high spirits, and received us with a cackling noise and much glee. Smith, in his turn, refreshed himself and prepared to depart. It was already dark, and I remember the wind howled fearfully, but he was determined to go in spite of everything, and even the remonstrances of his wife could not move him, and away we rattled. It was very dark, but the horse was perfectly acquainted with the road - I say the horse, because my master was so drunk that he could scarcely keep his seat. As far as my brother and myself were concerned we were snugly stowed away in a corner of the nondescript vehicle in which we rode, although both of us felt lost in fear and grief. We jogged along as well as the rough road would permit, my mistress, who was sitting beside me, having had frequent recourses to the bottle, at last fell asleep, and so continued until we arrived at the first turnpike gate. The custodian was asleep in bed, and did not stir until my master had called him several times, cursed him as many, and flung handfuls of beans, which he had in his overcoat pocket, at his window. when he did arouse the sleeper, he too, took a similar view of the interruption, sending to the d.....l all coaches, horses, gigs, and vehicles whatsoever.

After a tedious drive they reached Cotherstone, on the borders of the North Riding of Yorkshire, a few miles from Barnard Castle, and the narrative continues;

"There were about fifty boys. The building had formerly been a nunnery, and was built in the form of a square, with a courtyard in the centre, into which all the windows looked, The exterior presenting dead walls. There were two gates at opposite sides of the square, which were locked every night at eight o'clock, thus debarring all exit. On one side of the square was a playground, out of which we were not allowed to go more than once or twice a month, and into which we were turned on the morning after our arrival. Never shall I forget the heart-sinking I felt at the sight of the crowd of unhealthy young ragamuffins, with their hardend faces, who

48

surrounded us and treated us to jeers and laughter. Other realities of our situation were soon apparent: our clothes were taken from us, only to be returned on occasional Sundays when we attended church at the neighbouring village of Romaldkirk, and others of a workhouse quality substituted, while our shoes were replaced by wooden clogs. Our bed-rooms, three in number, were little better than granaries. In each room were fourteen or fifteen wooden beds with straw mattresses, and each with a couple of blankets. Our dining-room was a large gloomy apartment with an earthen floor, the only articles of furniture being long wooden benches, at which we stood and ate our miserable rations - yes, stood, for we had not even chairs. The schoolroom was a lofty chamber which I suppose had been the chapel. It had only one small stove and our suffering from cold in the winter was horrible. There were several large holes in the roof which let in water in rainy weather. We had two ruffians, who were styled teachers, beside our master, who seldom, or never entered the schoolroom but to assist at punishing as the ministers of the Holy Inquisition witnessed the tortures of their victims. We rose at five, and at eight were assembled in the dining chamber to breakfast. This consisted of black bread, milk, and water, and when finished, we repaired to the play-ground, and school commenced at nine. At one, we again assembled to dine. This meal was varied every day; milk and bread, then soup, a small tureen of it among twelve boys, with about an ounce of meat to each often in a putrid state. None of the teachers dined with us, they merely superintended the distribution of our often disgusting rations like huntsmen feeding a kennel of hounds, which is no bad resemblance to our dinner parties. At five we suppered off black bread and milk, played till seven and were then sent off to bed.

"Another regulation of this establishment was that no holidays were allowed, and fond parents as a consolation used to send from time to time hampers containing among other goods, biscuits and sweetmeats, which upon delivery were forthwith appropriated by the stronger young ruffians in the school."

Following the description of school life he proceeds to describe the effect of the ill-treatment;

"I shall now show the horrible effects, physically and morally, which hard treatment and bad living produced on us miserable scholars, many of us sons of respectable parents, whose hearts would have bled with anguish had they but known the situation of their children, in the cruel selfishness which takes possession of the human heart to the exclusion of

49

all feelings of humanity - even so it was with us, young as most of us were. The elder and stronger boys tyrannized in a brutal manner over the younger and weaker.

"As their own portions of food were too small to satisfy the cravings of hunger they compelled their younger fellows to hide a part of their scanty fare for their benefit. It was of no use that the little fellow pleaded hunger, and with tears in his eyes, begged of him to obey."

Finally, he sums up this "master's method of education as being based on the following lines, the term "principles" being obviously inapplicable;

"1. To establish a boarding school in some remote corner and out of the reach of human eye.

"2. To advertise in the newspapers and to procure certain persons as referees.

"3. To see that his scholars ere he took them should be provided with a good stock of clothing, etc.

"4. When he had got them firmly secured, to take away from them their fine clothes, etc., and substitute in their place corderoy, and feed them on the coarsest and cheapest food, add plenty of extras to the quarterly accounts, etc., so as to secure to himself plenty of profit.

"Such was the vagabond that called himself a Teacher of Youth, and to whose 'fatherly care' (as he expressed it) we were entrusted."

The boys were removed from their school after two years by an uncle who, finding himself in the area, called in to see his nephews. He was so horrified by what he saw that he withdrew them immediately.

Teaching methods in the schools were, to say the least, strange, and not just on Dickens' account. Here first, from 'Nicholas Nickleby' is how Squeers taught;

⸱   *"This is the first class in English spelling and philosophy, Nickleby," said Squeers, beckoning Nicholas to stand beside him. "We'll get up a Latin one, and hand that over to you. - Now, then, where's the first boy?"*

"Please, sir, he's cleaning the back parlour window,"said the temporary head of the philosophical class.

"So he is, to be sure," rejoined Squeers. "We go upon the practical mode of teaching, Nickleby - the regular education system. C-l-e-a-n, clean, verb active, to make bright, to scour. W-i-n, win, d-e-r, der, winder, as casement.

When the boy knows this out of book, he goes and does it. It's just the same principle as the use of the globes. - Where's the second boy?"

"Please, sir, he's weeding the garden," replied a small voice.

"To be sure," said Squeers, by no means disconcerted. "So he is. B-o-t, bot, t-i-n, tin, bottin, n-e-y, ney, bottinney, noun substantive,, a knowledge of plants. When he has learned that bottinney means a knowledge of plants, he goes and knows 'em. That's our system, Nickleby; what do you think of it?"

"It's a very useful one, at any rate," answered Nicholas.

"I believe you," rejoined Squeers, not remarking the emphasis of his usher. - "Third boy, what's a horse?"

"A beast, sir," replied the boy.

"So it is," said Squeer. - "Ain't it, Nickleby?"

"I believe there is no doubt of that, sir," answered Nicholas.

"Of course there isn't," said Squeers. "A horse is a quadruped, and quadruped's Latin for beast, as everybody that's gone through the grammar knows, or else where's the use of having grammars at all?"

"Where, indeed!" said Nicholas, abstractedly.

"As you're perfect in that," resumed Squeers, turning to the boy, "go and look after my horse, and rub him down well, or I'll rub you down. The rest of the class go and draw water up, till somebody tells you to leave off; for it's washing-day to-morrow, and they want the coppers filled."

So saying he dismissed the first class to their experiments in practical philosophy, and eyed Nicholas with a look, half cunning and half doubtful, as if he were not altogether certain what he might think of him by this time.'

No such account exists, to mu knowledge, of this kind of teaching at William Shaw's Academy, but, writing in 'The Dickensian' magazine in 1939, S.J. Rust demonstrated that Shaw's teaching methods in some subjects was unorthodox and clearly demonstrated a less-than-perfect knowledge of the field;

'The book used by W.C. Blanchard was devoted to Book-keeping, and the date of the entries is usually 1836. It begins with "Book-keeping by Single Entry, The Day Book." This would certainly not pass any accountant of to-day, for Dr. and Cr. entries follow one another in the same column without distinction, except the "Cr." or "Dr." written after each entry. The boy proudly announces the "End of the Day Book" and then plunges into the Ledger, which is properly kept. He

then proceeds to "Book-keeping by Double Entry," but after a few pages of the "Waste Book" the leaves have been removed.

As an example of beautiful writing and neat work, this book could hardly be surpassed. Every figure is perfectly formed. Every line is neatly ruled. The headings - some in Old English Text and others in "Copper Plate" - are perfectly written. As an example of practical book-keeping it is too wordy and cumbersome in method. We must remember, however, that Book-keeping was then less of an art than it is to-day. I should say that any business man would welcome W.C. Blanchard into his office.

The first of the two books written by John Blanchard was completed on April 21st 1835, and the second on July 4th 1837, so that we have an opportunity of judging progress in knowledge as well as in hand-writing.

The earlier book deals with Arithmetic - Alligation (prices of mixtures), Vulgar and Decimal Fractions, followed one another, to be succeeded by Square Root and simple Mensuration. At the close of the book are a number of simple examples in Practical Geometry, such as the bisecting of an angle, or the erection of a perpendicular.

In Arithmetic the plan of study was to copy out a rule and a few worked examples, with the same meticulous care and perfect calligraphy which characterised the work of W.C. Blanchard. The progress would appear to have been slow if one may judge from the date January 17th at the foot of one page and that of April 21st forty pages later.

When I first glanced at John Blanchard's second book, I thought we must allow William Shaw's claim to teach mathematics, for it begins with Logarithms and continues with Plane Trigonometry and Oblique Trigonometry (Solution of Triangles). Following this, having written boldly "The end of Oblique Trigonometry," the boy began Algebra with addition of 2a and 3a. It was then evident that the Logarithms and Trigonometry were merely copied from the Text-book. The rule used for finding the angles of a triangle when the sides are given was far more complex than that which we use to-day; yet the boy copied it correctly and copied two examples worked with the aid of Logarithmic Sines of five figures. That any boy could have done so intelligibly without having begun Algebra is out of the question; and the very order of the study shows that the master, himself, knew nothing of these subjects.

Before beginning Algebra the boy copied three pages of introductory matter, beginning with the delightful dictum: "Algebra is a kind of specious Arithmetic."

The books show that both boys possessed natural artistic ability. W.C. Blanchard has copied an old church gate with true appreciation; while John, besides surrounding his name with graceful swans, turns the right-angled triangle which illustrated an answer in Mensuration into a picturesque castle beside a stream. When he comes to make an original sketch of a house, however, the lack of perspective shows that the artistic talent was undirected.

There is not a single erasure nor a dirty finger mark in these three books. The perfection of neatness tells of strong discipline.'

The boys at Shaw's school often wrote letters home, but they do not ring true, even allowing for the fact that in 1818 there was far more formality than we see today. The language is not that of a child. Did Shaw, then, dictate what was to be written? Here are four letters from the same boy written between Boxing Day 1817 and the same date a year later;

Bowes, Dec. 26th, 1817

Honored Uncle,
With much pleasure I send you these few lines and hope this specimen of my writing, being my first, will please you. I am very well in health, and shall be glad to hear that you are the same. With love to my Mother and all my dear Relations
I remain
Your dutiful Nephew
John Cuthbert Dobson.

Bowes, Feb. 18th, 1818.

My dear Mother,
I send you my best thanks for your present of a cake, and shall do all I can to be a good boy and to make good improvement in my learning. I often think of you my dear Mother, and will always endeavour to please you. I am in good health and hope you are so too.
To you and my Aunt I send my love and am
My dear Mother
Your dutiful Son
John C. Dobson.

Bowes, August 15th, 1818.

Dear Mother,
I am sensible of the many obligations I am under to my dear Uncle and beg you to convey my acknowledgements to him in the best manner you can. His favors I will endeavour to deserve. To you I also return my thanks for the present you sent me by my good Master; and in the hopes that you

and my kind Uncle are well and happy, I am
affectionately
Dear Mother,
Your dutiful Son
John C. Dobson.

Bowes, December 26th, 1818.

Dear Mother,
Christmas here, is a time of many pleasures; but the greatest pleasure I feel is that of writing to you. I am quite well in health and very happy, and hope you and all my relations join me in those blessings. My master will be in London in a few days, upon a three weeks' visit. I continue to get on as fast as possible in my learning and like my school very well. In love to you and all my relations, hoping you will have a pleasant Christmas and a happy New Year,
I am
Dear Mother,
Your dutiful Son,
John. C. Dobson.
P.S. - Mr. and Mrs. Shaw send you their respectful compliments.
N.B. - Mr. Shaw's intention, this Christmas, is to wait at Mr. Bulman's, from 12 to 2 o'clock, daily, to receive the applications of his friends.

Three months later this little nine year old boy, John Cuthbert Dobson, son of a widow in London, was buried on March 16th, 1818 in Bowes churchyard. Shaw paid R. Braithwaite £3-6-11d for 'stone, workmanship and lettering' for a headstone for the boy, but he received his receipt for the money on 16th September, 1819. Had he been tardy in settling the account? On the account for the gravestone were the following lines, presumably the poor boy's epitaph which Braithwaite had carved;

The youth who lies beneath this tomb
Was like a flower to sight,
When Death quick Blighted all his bloom
And closed his eyes in night;
In vain affection heaves the sigh
In vain is grief pourtray'd.
Every youth was born to die
Every flower to fade.

Burials at Bowes

In whatever light one pictures the man William Shaw and his ethics, there is incontrovertible evidence that a great many of the pupils at schools in the Parish of Bowes died during their time there. Shaw had between 250 and 300 pupils at his school, and there were several other schools. The following list covers a period of seventy five years and Shaw does not seem to have had more deaths than the other headmasters. The list does make pathetic reading, but if this is the full total of deaths, it averages out at less than one a year in times when health and medical care were much poorer than they are today. What we do not, of course, know is how many boys died and were buried elsewhere by their parents. This list is of burials, not deaths. Nor do we know how many pupils left the schools in a state of ill-health and subsequently died at home.

Here then is the dreadful list of burials in the Parish of Bowes between 1759 and 1834;

2 Apr 1759	(blank) A boy at Mr. Lamb School.
11 Dec 1764	Thomas Abbott from London. A Scholar at Bowes.
11 Dec 1764	Benjamin Sherwood another Scholar at Bowes, both Scholars at Mr. Jackson school.
24 Mar 1765	Benjamin Logon from London. A Scholar at Mr. Jackson School at Bowes.
13 June 1765	Joseph Brockell One of Mr. Jackson Scholars.
23 Oct 1765	William Marsh one of Jackson Scholars.
3 Apr 1767	John Piggot. A boy of Taylors School.
26 Jan 1771	Charles Jeynes Mr. Jackson's Scholar.
29 Jan 1771	John Wilson Mr. Jackson's Scholar.
15 Apr 1771	William Canon Mr. Richd Jackson's Scholar, Bowes.
8 May 1771	John Howis Mr. Richd Jackson's Scholar, Bowes.
21 May 1771	William Todd Scholar of Mr. Richard Jackson, Bowes.
9 June 1773	John Deacon Bowes, Mr. Taylor's Scholar.
7 Jan 1774	Joseph Constable Mr. Taylor's School, Bowes.
15 Nov 1777	John Cursil Mr. George Taylor's Scholar, Bowes.
27 June 1785	Joseph Stones a Scholar of Mr. Johnson, Gilmonby.
28 Oct 1788	John Clements Mr. Dotes Scholar, Hullands.
30 May 1789	Thomas Wilson a Scholar of Mr. Dotes, Hullands.
25 Feb 1791	John Pearl Mr. Dotes Scholar, Bowes.
7 Jan 1792	John Morely, Bowes, Mr. Dotes Scholar.
17 Jan 1793	William Walford Dess Sir William Walford Dess, of Vicarage Lane, Stratford, Essex, Mr. Dotes Scholar, Bowes.
18 Apr 1793	William Brown Mr. Dotes Scholar, Bowes.
11 May 1793	George Demer Mr. Dotes Scholar, Bowes.
14 June 1797	Stephen Riddick who was a Scholar with Mr. Thornborrow.
23 July 1798	Joseph Daniel a Scholar with Mr. Thornborrow.

18 Nov 1798	William Wetherstone Scholar at George Frederick Dotes Academy.
11 Dec 1798	Robert Dourne of Edward Johnson's School, Gilmonby.
12 Dec 1799	Henry Dogherty Scholar with Mr. Thornborrow.
26 Apr 1801	(blank) Scholar at Mr. Horn's.
4 July 1803	George Grinville Scholar at Jonathan Horns.
2 Feb 1804	Richard Scott a Scholar with Mr. Joseph Lambert.
4 May 1804	Timothy Draught Scholar with Mr. Chapman.
7 May 1804	Thomas Heppel Scholar with Mr. Chapman.
20 May 1804	George Welchon a Scholar with ye revd Jos Adamthwaite.
13 June 1804	Henry Wallis Scholar with Mr. Chapman.
25 July 1805	George Hunt a Scholar of the Revd Jos Lambert.
24 May 1806	William Mackelly Mr. Lamberts boy.
10 Apr 1808	Andrew Murphy Vannine a School Boy.
10 Oct 1810	Robert Wray a native of London, a Scholar at Mr. John Adamthwaites School in Bowes aged 10.
22 Sept 1811	Henry Hickes a Scholar at Mr. John Adamthwaite's School here. s Francis Hickes of Old Ford in the Parish of St. Mary Stratford in the County of Middlesex aged 10 years.
16 Apr 1812	William Wilson a Scholar (at the School of Messrs. Shaw and Wilson). A Native of London aged 12.
10 Sept 1812	John Robinson a Native of the West Indies, a Scholar at Mr. Adamthwaite's School in Bowes - aged 11
26 Mar 1814	Benjamin Hooper Bowes, aged 9. s. Benjamin of Essendon Bury, Herts. Farmer, a Scholar at Mr. Adamthwaite's School.
8 June 1814	Joseph Thornhill a Native of London aged 11, a Scholar at Mr. Shaw's School.
29 Nov 1814	John Burgess. A native of London aged 12. a Scholar at Mr. Shaw's School, Bowes.
29 Dec 1814	William Jecks Digby & Ruth Jecks of the Victuallers Office, Somerset Place, London. A Scholar at Mr. Adamthwaite's School, aged 12.
4 May 1815	Luke Hardman a Scholar at Mr. George Clarkson's School, Bowes. aged 15.
8 May 1815	John Clarkson, son of Mr. George Clarkson.
7 June 1816	George Johns a Scholar at Mr. Horn's School, Gilmonby, supposed 13 years.
3 Nov 1816	William Bennell s Mr. Bennell, No 111 Fleet Street, London. Scholar at Mr. Horn's School, Gilmonby Hall, aged 12.
10 Nov 1816	William Cox s William Cox of Wood Street, Old Street Road, London. A Scholar at Mr. Adamthwaite's School, aged 10.
15 Dec 1816	Frederick Tyers s the late Robert Tyers, London. A Scholar at Mr. Horn's School, Gilmonby, age 9.

The children at their cousin's grave.

9 Jan 1817	John Julian s George Julian. London. A̅ Scholar at Mr. Horn's School, Gilmonby, age 7.
9 Feb 1817	Henry Needham s Mr. Needham, Hackney near London. A Scholar at Mr. Horn's School. age 10.
28 Dec 1817	John Winch Evance a Scholar at Mr. Horn's School age 11.
16 Mar 1819	John Cuthbert Dobson s Mary. Widow. London. A Scholar at Mr. Shaw's School, Bowes, age 9.
18 Oct 1820	John White a Scholar at Mr. Shaw's School, Bowes. age 10.
23 Mar 1821	John Branscomb a Scholar at Mrs. Adamthwaite School, Bowes. late s William Branscomb of London. age 12.
28 June 1821	Henry Shepherd Bracken a Scholar at Mr. Shaw's School, s Lancelot Bracken of London, age 9.
28 July 1821	John Bell a Scholar at Mr. Horn's School, Gilmonby supposed a Native of Newcastle, aged 8.
19 Oct 1821	William Ceal Crow a Scholar at Mr. Clarkson's School, s R.F. Crow of Calcutta in the East Indies, age 7.
20 Oct 1821	William Linnage a Scholar at Mrs. Adamthwaite's School, from Godmanchester near Huntingdon, age 11.
2 Mar 1822	William Britt Scholar at Mr. Horn's School, Gilmonby, age 12.
29 Mar 1822	John Henry Symes from London. Scholar at Mr. Shaw's School, age 11.
17 Apr 1822	Owen Bach a Scholar of Mrs. Adamthwaite's School, Bowes, s Revd Edward Bach, Ostend, age 9.
14 July 1822	Frederick George Geddes, Scholar at Mr. Shaw's School, age 9.
7 Feb 1826	George Brooks of Chatteris in the County of Cambridgeshire; aged 9
19 Dec 1826	Thomas Foster a Scholar of Mr. Shaw's, Bowes, age 18.
20 Mar 1831	Richard Taylor Bowes, a boy at Mr. Shaw's, age 10.
20 Mar 1834	Francis Lees, Ealing, Middlesex, Mr. Shaw's Scholar age 12

In this list it becomes obvious that Shaw's school had no greater death rate than the other schools. It must also be taken into account that there were sometimes epidemics in the villages which affected the schools. In order to avoid a long catalogue of names becoming just another list of statistics, and having already quoted some letters from the young John Cuthbert Dobson, here are two letters relating to another boy whose name appears on the list, George Brooks.

Dear Parents,

I write you these few lines to inform you on Saturday, 5th of November, we had a jovial and merry day and night in burning old Guy upon the hills, and I am happy to say without one of my schoolfellows happening any misfortune whatever, and I am glad to say I have enjoyed the best of health since I last wrote to you, which I hope is the same with you and all my dear Brothers and Sisters, Uncles, Aunts and Cousins and all my other dear Relations. I may truly say neither Masters Clarke or Bonfields have ailed any thing whatever, neither have I seen a doctor since I came here.

I feel very happy and comfortable and have been so ever since I came. Tell Masters Sumner and Bonfields we had roast Geese and giblet pies as usual last week. I like the country very well, and last week we had some sliding without any accident. I hope by this time all my friends and relations are perfectly well again, to whom I beg you will make our kindest respects; we will all write separately next month by our Master, who the latter end of it intends going to London and remaining about three weeks, and will inform you when he returns, that any parcel may be brought us. I have 10 s. left of my money, but my Master thinks I had better wear my shoes sliding than skates, for fear of a misfortune by them.

I now beg to remain in love and duty to yourselves not forgetting Mr. and Mrs. Shaws compliments who are very kind to me.

Your affectionate Son

George Brooks.

....

Bowes, Feby 2nd, 1826.

Dear Sir,

It is with feelings indescribable, I again inform you respecting your dear boy, who I am sorry to say continues gradually hastening away from us, and I am afraid my next letter will have to state his final departure, as this morning he has begun with convulsion fits, and has not left us any hope; the feelings of a Parent I can bear with having experienced a loss myself, but I hope and trust on receipt of this or yesterday's letter you will immediately come to our house, and arrange as you think proper, which will be much more satisfactory and very relieve us. This I would not have considered anything an impediment, provided it would have been useful to him, as I must say, he always attracted my *particular attention being so very peaceable and clean in his person.*

In hopes of seeing you on Sunday, and that Mrs. Brooks and yourself may long be spared to each other.

> *I am, Dear Sir,*
> *Your hble Servt*
> *Wm. Shaw.*

Mr. Brooks.
  Chatteris.
    Isle of Ely.
      Cambridgeshire.

In the margin of the letter, is written in pencil, 'the boy George Brooks died 10.55 p.m. the same night.'

The boy was buried five days later, but whether his parents came up to Bowes to see Shaw we do not know.

William Shaw in Court

On his first full day in Barnard Castle, Charles Dickens had heard about the court case in which William Shaw had been involved, but he had only a brief outline of what had transpired on that occasion. He therefore made an entry in his diary and followed it up later. He knew that the trial had taken place between 1823 and 1826.

The trial, or, rather, trials, actully took place on Thursday, October 30th and Friday, October 31st, 1823, in the Court of Common Pleas. The two cases tried were 'Jones versus Shaw' and 'Ocherby versus Shaw'. In some reports of the trial, the name was spelt 'Ockerby'. This is a contemporary account taken from a Yorkshire newspaper which printed the story under the headline;

'CRUELTY OF A SCHOOLMASTER'

Jones versus Shaw

This was an action brought to recover damages of a schoolmaster in Yorkshire on account of the injury done to the health of two sons of the plaintiff, one of whom was alleged to have lost his sight from the negligence of the defendant.

Mr. Sergeant Vaughan stated the case. It appeared that Mr. Shaw kept a seminary at Bowes, near Greta Bridge in Yorkshire, and advertised to teach young gentlemen, reading, writing, arithmetic, Latin and Greek, with board, clothes and lodgings for £20 per annum. The plaintiff sent his two sons, Richard and William, in October 1819 to the establishment at Bowes. Sometime after being there, William was attacked with bad eyes and eventually lost his sight.

This boy gave the following evidence on the trial. Witness will be twelve years old in January; could see as well as any person when he went to Mr. Shaw's school; he had small pox a year before, but it did not affect his eyes. The first week he was treated very well; he got toast and tea for breakfast, but they then turned him among the rest of the boys and gave him hasty-pudding for breakfast; for dinner the boys had meat and potatoes on Sunday, and on other days bread and cheese: when any gentlemen came to see their children, Mr. Shaw used to come down and tell the boys who had not their jackets and trousers on to get under the table and hide themselves; the boys were frequently without a jacket or trousers; they washed in a large trough; there were only two towels for all the boys, which the big boys used to pre-occupy; their supper consisted of warm milk and water and bread, which was called tea; five boys generally slept in a bed; his brother and three boys slept with him; there were thirty beds in the room; in some beds there were only three

61

or four boys; every morning the boys used to flea the beds for which purpose they were provided with quills by the ushers, and if they did not catch all the fleas they were beaten. On Sunday they had pot skimmings for tea, in which there was vermin; the ushers offered a penny for every maggot, but on their being found the ushers would not pay them. About nine months after he had been to the school, his sight was affected; he could not see to write his copy, and Mr. Shaw threatened to beat him; the next day he could not see at all, and Mr. Shaw sent him to the washhouse, as he had no doctor, and he would not have him in his room; there were eighteen boys there besides himself, of whom two were totally blind. In November, he was quite blind and was then sent to a private room where there were nine other boys blind, a doctor was sent for, but he had no medical aid in the washhouse; the doctor (Benning) then discharged him, saying 'that he was blind of one eye, but could see with the other'. Dr. Benning used to come to the school when the boys had nearly lost their sight. He merely looked at the boys' eyes, and turned them off; he gave them no physic or eye-water, or anything else. There was no difference in his fare during his illness, or his health. Mr. Shaw occasionally saw him but gave him no assistance. The same number of boys slept in his bed during his illness as before.

Richard Jones corroborated the statement of his brother, adding, that he had the itch all the time he was there; twenty other boys laboured under the same disorder.

Two boys who had each lost one eye, and one quite blind were also examined. Benjamin Clatton described the mode of flea-hunting; there was a quill to each bed, which the several bed-fellows filled and emptied into the fire.

Mr. Tyrrel and Mr. Lawrence, two medical gentlemen, deposed that the cause of these boys' blindness was gross neglect.

Mr. Sergeant Pell, for the defence, said he was prepared to show that Mr. and Mrs. Shaw evinced the most tender regard for the pupils of the school; that Mr. Shaw's life had been endangered through the anxiety he felt to eradicate the disease out of the school, and that although the boys paid the small amount of twenty pounds a year for their board and education, yet when the disease broke out, and could not be restrained by the ordinary medical aid of the neighbourhood, he employed the most eminent oculist in the metropolis (Sir W. Adams) and gave him 300 guineas to leave London and go down to Bowes.

Mr. Benning, Sir W. Adams and other witnesses were then called. The first described the treatment of the complaint, which Sir. W. Adams deposed to be judicious.

Verdict for the plaintiff; damages £300.

Another action was brought against Mr. Shaw on Friday (October 31st), by the father of a boy called Ocherby, who also lost his sight at the school, and damages to the same amount were given.'

The Ocherby/Shaw case is not well-documented in the newspaper account. The gist of it was that in the June or July of 1820, Mr. Ocherby had sent three sons to Shaw's school. By the September of that year two were badly affected by ophthalmia. In January, 1821, the boys' father went to see Shaw on one of his visits to London and asked why he had received no letters. He did not, at that time, know anything about the eye infection, and Shaw told him that they had a slight disorder in their eyes brought on by their standing too near the bonfire on November 5th. Actually, the two lads were already too blind to either read or write, and one had lost an eye.

There can be little doubt that the disease was spread by infected towels and washing facilities. Only two towels for so many boys was preposterous, and Shaw did not refute the boy's evidence. Precisely what form the infection took is not known, but it was obviously a most contagious condition and not just a dietary deficiency, and so there are several possibilities.

One disease far more common in the 1820's than it is now was 'pink-eye', which was often found in schools. Medically-speaking, it was caused by the Kochs-Weeks bacillus and infection was spread by contact with contaminated basins, communal towels, and water. The washing facilities which appear to have been provided at Bowes Academy at the time were perfect for such a disease to spread very quickly. Nor would the condition retreat if the patient was otherwise debilitated by being fed an inadequate diet. It is not generally known, but Shaw owned several farms in and around Bowes. However, how much of the fresh food grown there reached the mouths of his pupils is not known, but the evidence would suggest very little of it.

The other possible disease was Trachoma, which is a serious form of conjunctivitis. This is highly contagious and is caused by a virus which can be transmitted through the bodies of lice. It is regarded as such a serious complaint because it produces corneal ulcers and scars, and affects both eyes. It recurs easily and can damage vision severely, pariculiarly if not treated quickly. It is rare in this country now but was rife two hundred years ago in Egypt and the East and was brought to this country by soldiers returning from the Napoleonic Wars, just a few years before the Shaw trials. It should be stressed that these are just two of the many possible causes of blindness at Shaw's school.

He was fined £600 altogether to which had to be added the cost of the eye specialist and his own defence costs; the financial cost was enormous for those days, and on top of this his reputation suffered. He must have lost some custom as a result of these legal actions. It should be pointed out that to tolerate such losses and still stay in business,

Shaw must have been a wealthy man; he must also have recovered fairly quickly because when Dickens ventured north fifteen years later, he found him at the head of a thriving establishment.

Dickens had obviously read the account of the trial before he wrote the following in Chapter 7 of the novel. Nicholas is being packed off to bed on his first night at Dotheboys Hall;

   ‘   *"I'll come in myself and show you where the well is, " said Squeers. "You'll always find a bit of soap in the kitchen window; that belongs to you."*

     "I don't know, I'm sure," he said, "whose towel to put you on; but if you'll make shift with something tomorrow morning, Mrs. Squeers will arrange that in the course of the day. My dear, don't forget."

     "I'll take care," replied Mrs. Squeers; "and mind you take care, young man, and get first wash. The teacher ought always to have it; but they always get the better of him if they can."

William Shaw, Family Man

Although much research has been done into the subject, little is known of William Shaw's background. He was born in London but where, precisely is not known. Since he was fifty-five when Dickens met him in 1838, he must have been born in 1782 or 1783. We do not know when or why he came to Bowes but he probably came with money of his own since in 1812 he was in partnership with the Vicar of Bowes, Richard Wilson, and together they ran a school. Wilson was incumbent of the Church of St. Giles in Bowes from 1810 to 1822. There seems to be no record of the school having been run by Wilson alone, since it is recorded in the Parish Records of Bowes as 'Messrs. Shaw and Wilson's School, Bowes' in 1812. Wilson had come to Bowes from Whorlton. T.P. Cooper suggests that Wilson was at least a sleeping partner in the business until his death in 1822, but the Parish Records show that in 1814 Mr. Shaw was the sole proprietor of his own school. This information is consolidated by the burial records which record a native of London, William Wilson having been at the school of Messrs. Shaw and Wilson, but after 1814 all the burials say simply 'at Mr. Shaw's school.'

On the subject of William Shaw's qualifications to teach, no evidence has yet been unearthed to show that he was a graduate of Oxford, Cambridge or Durham, the only three universities at that time. None of the Barnard Castle masters listed any academic qualifications in their advertisements.

Shaw had come to Bowes before 1812, however, so we can assume that he was teaching in some other establishment. On 24th November 1810 he married Bridget Laidman of Bowes. She was probably born in February, 1784, for a baptism is recorded of Biddy Laidman on 21st February, 1784. The Laidmans were an old Bowes family, but how wealthy they were, or otherwise is not known. One must speculate about whether Shaw married for money. Biddy was the daughter of Jonathan and Mary Laidman. Officiating at the Shaw wedding was the new incumbent of Bowes, Richard Wilson who married the couple by licence. The bride was unable to write and simply signed with an X.

William Shaw must have known happiness and sadness in his personal life for the couple had a large family not all of whom lived long.

Their first child, Mary Ann Shaw was baptised on 21st September 1811. She married John Bousfield, a wealthy yeoman farmer, and their daughter Mary, who was born in 1852, had a very unhappy childhood when she was taunted with the nickname, 'Fanny Squeers'. It was she who in 1896 had a window to her grandfather's memory put in Bowes church. The window was not inserted by public subscription, as is generally thought.

On 1st August 1813 the Shaws had a son, William, but he died at the age of 24 and was buried on October 27th, 1837 in Bowes churchyard, just a few weeks before Dickens' visit. Could this sad event have been responsible for Shaw's curt reception of the author?

The next child, Jane, only lived to the age of four. Baptised on January 21st 1816, she was buried on 31st May, 1820.

Next came another son, Jonathan Shaw, baptised on March 26th 1818.

Just before the death of Jane Shaw, another son had been born. He was Thomas Laidman Shaw who was baptised on May 11th, 1820.

Having lost one daughter called Jane, the Shaws named their next daughter, born in August 1822, Jane.

Three years later, in 1825, came Emmily, and, two years after that, twins. They were John and Eliza, baptised just before Christmas in 1827, but Eliza lived only eleven weeks and was buried on March 1st, 1828.

It has always been maintained that William Shaw was held in high esteem by local people. He was an educated man but it must not be forgotten that as a landowner and provider for about three hundred boys he was a force to be reckoned with. He had money to spend and local tradesmen would have been unwise to offend him.

Boys who attended his school, admittedly many years after his trial, refused to believe any evil of their headmaster.

Smike

One of the most pathetic characters in all of Dickens' novels is Smike, who appears in 'Nicholas Nickleby.'

Dickens himself describes how the character came into his mind. Talking of his visit to Bowes in the letter to Mrs. S.C. Hall, he writes;

'There is an old church near the school, and the first gravestone I stumbled on that dreary winter afternoon was placed above the grave of a boy, eighteen long years old, who had died suddenly, the inscription said. I suppose his heart broke - the camel falls down 'suddenly' when they heap the last load upon his back - died at that wretched place. I think his ghost put Smike into my mind upon the spot.'

There are many appearances of Smike in the novel and he is the epitome of the ill-treatment received by boys at the hands of Squeers. Here Nicholas encounters the poor wretch;

'As he was absorbed in these meditations, he all at once encountered the upturned face of Smike, who was on his knees before the stove, picking a few stray cinders from the hearth and planting them on the fire. He had paused to steal a look at Nicholas, and when he saw that he was observed, shrunk back, as if expecting a blow.

"You need not fear me," said Nicholas, kindly. "Are you cold?"

"N-n-o."

"You are shivering."

"I am not cold," replied Smike, quickly. "I'm used to it."

There was such an obvious fear of giving offence in his manner, and he was such a timid, broken-spirited creature, that Nicholas could not help exclaiming, "Poor fellow!"

If he had struck the drudge, he would have slunk away without a word; but now he burst into tears.

"Oh dear, oh dear!" he cried, covering his face with his cracked and horny hands. "My heart will break - it will, it will!"

"Hush!" said Nicholas, laying his hand upon his shoulder. "Be a man; you are nearly one by years, God help you."

"By years!" cried Smike. "Oh dear, dear, how many of them! How many of them since I was a little child, younger than any that are here now! Where are they all?"

"Whom do you speak of?" inquired Nicholas, wishing to rouse the poor half-witted creature to reason. "Tell me."

"My friends," he replied, "myself - my- oh, what sufferings mine have been!"

"There is always hope," said Nicholas; he knew not what to say.

"No," rejoined the other, "no, none for me. Do you remember the boy that died here?"

Nicholas instructs Smike in the art of acting.

"I was not here, you know," said Nicholas, gently; "but what of him?"

"Why," replied the youth, drawing closer to his questioner's side, "I was with him at night, and when it was all silent he cried no more for friends he wished to come and sit with him, but began to see faces round his bed that came from home; he said they smiled, and talked to him, and he died at last lifting his head to kiss them. Do you hear?"

"Yes, yes," rejoined Nicholas.

"What faces will smile on me when I die?" cried his companion, shivering. "Who will talk to me in those long nights? They cannot come from home; they would frighten me if they did, for I don't know what it is, and shouldn't know them. Pain and fear, pain and fear for me, alive or dead. No hope, no hope!"

The bell rang to bed; and the boy subsiding at the sound into his usual listless state, crept away as if anxious to avoid notice.'

In 1877, two ladies took a holiday in Teesdale where they met a man who claimed to have been a pupil at Shaw's school.

'Ye'll a seen Dotheboy's Hall? Ay, there were four o' them schools afore that book war written, but it war all up wi' em after.'

The ladies asked if Dickens' account had not been exaggerated. The man replied,

'Why yes, it war a leetle, but there war a deal o' truth in it.'

He went on to recount how he had swallowed copious amounts of brimstone and treacle, and that he knew Smike who was then living some twelve miles distant. He went on,

'Ye know, he war rayther touched here. I got him one day to weed a bed o'carrots, and he pulled carrots and weeds up altogether.'

At Darlington

On his return journey to London on the Saturday, Dickens had to change coaches at Darlington. He chanced to pick up a copy of the Durham Advertiser. In it he was amazed to read an article about himself. It ran as follows;

'   *"Brief Autobiography of Boz. - As part of the uncertainty of literary remuneration (says Dr. Mackenzie, the Liverpool correspondent of the 'New York Star') I would instance the example of 'Boz'. When he commenced the Pickwick Papers he was living on five guineas a week, as reporter on the 'Morning Chronicle.' Chapman and Hall having with some difficulty, been persuaded to become the Pickwick publishers, agreed to give him ten pounds a month for each number, or £120, for the whole work. After the second number, the sale became so immense as to induce the publishers to give him £70 a month; and since number 10, he has had one half of the profits, including those of the first numbers. By the Pickwick Papers alone he will net between £2000. and £3000. Nor is this all; he was paid two guineas for Watkins Tottle and for 'Sketches by Boz,' which appeared in the 'Morning Chronicle.' For a column of such sketches he would have ten guineas from any magazine. He has, of course, cut reporting, and instead of some £300. a year, which he made 18 months ago, is in the receipt of at least £3000. To ensure him exclusively for himself, Mr. Bentley, the publisher, allows Mr. Dickens the sum of £1000. a year as editor of 'Bentley's Miscellany,' and twenty guineas per sheet also for whatever he writes in it. This is turning a popular name to good account."'*

Naturally Dickens penned a reply;

Darlington. / Saturday Morning.
Sir,

Waiting in this place for a York coach this morning, I chanced in the course of the few minutes I stayed here, to take up your paper of January the 26th. in which I saw a brief Autobiography of myself by Dr. Mackenzie. Dr. Mackenzie whoever he may be, knows as much of me as of the meaning of the word autobiography, in proof of which may I beg you to state on my authority that when I commenced the Pickwick Papers I was not living on five guineas a week as a Reporter on the Morning Chronicle - that Messrs. Chapman and Hall were never persuaded with some difficulty to become the Pickwick publishers but on the contrary first became known to me by waiting on me to propose the work - that no such pecuniary arrangement as the paragraph describes ever existed between us - that by the Pickwick Papers alone I have not netted between £2000 and £3000 - that the Sketch called Watkins Tottle never appear in the Morning Chronicle - that I am not now in the receipt of £3000 a year, and that Mr. Bentley does not give me £1000 a year for editing the Miscellany and twenty guineas a sheet for what I write in it.

I have the honor to be Sir
Your most obedt. Servant
CHARLES DICKENS.

To
The Editor of
The Durham Advertiser.'

An interesting footnote to this brief correspondence is that in 1870 the same Robert Shelton Mackenzie published a 'Life of Charles Dickens' and although it was full of mistakes it did contain some new information on Dickens' life.

In Conclusion

One hundred and fifty years have elapsed since Charles Dickens came north to expose to public scrutiny the iniquities of the Yorkshire schools. The question which has continually been asked since the publication of 'Nicholas Nickleby' is how accurately Dickens reflected the true state of affairs with regard to the schools. I must confess that, having thoroughly examined all the evidence I could unearth, I am led to the conclusion that although there were undoubtedly malpractices in those schools, or at least in some of them, Dickens nevertheless villified the establishments in a ruthless manner. It is said that the pen is mightier than the sword, and a pen in the hand of Charles Dickens proved to be one of the most formidable weapons known to Man. Moreover, Dickens had an unassailable platform on which to wield his weapon. His books were read by millions, the vast majority of whom accepted his words as the undisputable truth. What we need to know is why he dealt with William Shaw so severely. Why did he paint him as a contemptible rogue not fit to exist alongside respectable human beings? The evidence suggests that he barely met the man. Why, then, was he so ready to pillary and lampoon him on the basis of a trial and the word of others?

As far as can be ascertained, the solicitor, Barnes, had no 'axe to grind', but this was certainly not so in the case of McKay, the master dismissed by Shaw. He, no doubt, had every reason to hate his former employer. Why did he need to set up his own establishment in Barnard Castle? There were many other schools in the area. Would they not employ him? Did Shaw see to it that he could not find employment elsewhere? If Shaw did force him out of the local school system, what had he done to deserve such treatment? We must not allow ourselves to lose sight of the possibility that he fully deserved to be dismissed.

Unlike some earlier writers on this subject, I have tried not to assign blame or pronounce guilt, rather bring to light in one volume all the facts of the case.

There have been those who have argued that Dickens' pride was dented when Shaw refused him proper admission to his school. Was Dickens really so petty? There can be no doubt that Dickens had it firmly in his head that Shaw was one of the most evil of the Yorkshire schoolmasters and since he found no evidence to dissuade him from this view, he adhered to it and used his freedom as an author to add to his convictions.

I have already argued that the only real evidence against Shaw was the trial of 1823 and even then we must surely allow that it was pure ignorance and not cruelty which caused Shaw to take the course of action he did in isolating the boys in the wash-house. I feel that until new and more positive evidence comes to light, as it may yet well do, we must be very careful of assigning to William Shaw an amalgam of wrongs perpetrated in the dozen or so schools in the area. Why should Shaw, who had 'carried the can' for the last century and a half continue to do so when the actual evidence against him is, if we are honest, so slight.

Dickens claimed that his Squeers was the representative of a class and not a particular person, but we must deduce from his intimate knowledge of the law that he was here covering himself in case of any legal retribution. Nor in any of his letters does Dickens deliberately free any individual schoolmaster from guilt.

The case for and against William Shaw will no doubt continue to be debated for many more years. His school accounted for no more deaths of boys than did the others in the parish. Shaw's advertisement for his school did include the phrase "No Vacations" and he does thus attract the suggestion that his establishment was a semi prison for unwanted children. His teaching ability, certainly in mathematics is suspect but beyond that we can say little against him.

He was extremely good to his own children and educated one as a doctor. We do not know a great deal about what happened to him after the publication of 'Nicholas Nickleby', but he seems to have survived comfortably. The Yorkshire schools came to a rapid end after the book's publication and it is now difficult even to trace the sites of them all.

Today, one of England's finest public schools exists at Barnard Castle. Called Barnard Castle School it has a great reputation as a bastion of scholarship and a producer of upright young men, a great contrast with the Yorkshire schools which came to an end, to all intents and purposes, as Victoria's reign dawned.

The last words in this book should come from Dickens, and he obligingly provided them at the end of 'Nicholas Nickleby'. Nicholas returns to Yorkshire, where justice is not only done but is seen to be done. He travels north. Again, it is winter.

'The next morning he began his journey. It was now cold winter weather: forcibly recalling to his mind under what circumstances he had first travelled that road, and how many vicissitudes and changes he had since undergone. He was alone inside, the greater part of the way, and sometimes, when he had fallen into a doze, and, rousing himself, looked out of the window, and recognised some place which he well remembered as having passed, either on his journey down, or in the long walk back with poor Smike, he could hardly believe but that all which had since happened had been a dream, and that they were still plodding wearily on towards London, with the world before them.

To render these recollections the more vivid, it came on to snow as night set in; and, passing through Stamford and Grantham, and by the little alehouse, where he had heard the story of the bold Baron of Grogzwig, everything looked as if he had seen it but yesterday and not even a flake of the white crust on the roofs had melted away. Encouraging the train of ideas which flocked upon him, he could almost persuade himself that he sat again outside the coach, with Squeers and the boys; that he heard their voices in the air; and that he felt again, but with a mingled sensation of pain and pleasure now, the old sinking of the heart, and longing after home. While he

The breaking up at Dotheboys Hall.

was yet yielding himself up to these fancies he fell asleep, and dreaming of Madeline, forgot them.

He slept at the inn at Greta Bridge, on the night of his arraival, and, rising at a very early hour next morning, walked to the market town, and inquired for John Browdie's house. John lived in the outskirts, now he was a family man; and, as everybody knew him, Nicholas had no difficulty in finding a boy who undertook to guide him to his residence.

Dismissing his guide at the gate, and in his impatience not even stopping to admire the thriving look of cottage or garden either, Nicholas made his way to the kitchen door, and knocked lustily with his stick.

"Halloa!" cried a voice inside. "Waat be the matther noo? Be the toon a-fire? Ding, but thou mak'st noise eneaf!"

With these words, John Browdie opened the door himself, and opening his eyes too, to their utmost width, cried, as he clapped his hands together, and burst into a heart roar:

"Ecod, it be the godfeyther, it be the godfeyther! Tilly, here be Misther Nickleby. Gi' us thee hond, mun. Coom awa', coom awa'. In wi' 'un, doon beside the fire; tak' a soop o' thot. Dinnot say a word till thou'st droonk it a'! Oop wi' it, mun. Ding! but I'm reeght glod to see thee."

Adapting his action to his text, John dragged Nicholas into the kitchen, forced him down upon a huge settle beside a blazing fire, poured out from an enormous bottle about a quarter of a pint of spirits, thrust it into his hand, opened his mouth and threw back his head as a sign to him to drink it instantly, and stood with a broad grin of welcome overspreading his great red face, like a jolly giant.

"I might ha' knowa'd," said John, "that nobody but thou would ha' coom wi' sike a knock as yon. Thot was the wa' thou knocked at schoolmeasther's door, eh? Ha, ha, ha! But I say; waa't be a' this aboot schoolmeasther?"

"You know it then?" said Nicholas.

"They were talking aboot it, doon toon, last neeght," replied John, "but neane on 'em seemed quite to un'erstan' it loike."

"After various shiftings and delays," said Nicholas, "he has been sentenced to be transported for seven years, for being in the unlawful possession of a stolen will; and, after that, he has to suffer the consequence of a conspiracy."

"Whew!" cried John, "a conspiracy! Soomat in the pooder plot wa'? Eh? Soomat in the Guy Faux line?"

"No, no, no, a conspiracy connected with his school; I'll explain it presently."

"Thot's reeght!" said John, "explain it arter breakfast, not noo, for thou bee'st hoongry, and so am I; and Tilly she mun' be at the bottom o' a' explanations, for she says thot's

the mutual confidence. Ha, ha, ha! Ecod it's a room start, is the mutual confidence!"

The entrance of Mrs. Browdie, with a smart cap on and very many apologies for their having been detected in the act of breakfasting in the kitchen, stopped John in his discussion of this grave subject, and hastened the breakfast: which, being composed of vast mounds of toast, new-laid eggs, boiled ham, Yorkshire pie, and other cold substantials (of which heavy relays were constantly appearing from another kitchen under the direction of a very plump servant), was admirably adapted to the cold bleak morning, and received the utmost justice from all parties. At last, it came to a close. and the fire which had been lighted in the best parlour having by this time burnt up, they adjourned thither, to hear what Nicholas had to tell.

Nicholas told them all, and never was there a story which awakened so many emotions in the breasts of two eager listeners. At one time, honest John groaned in sympathy, and at another roared with joy; at one time he vowed to go up to London on purpose to get a sight of the Brothers Cheeryble; at another, swore that Tim Linkinwater should receive such a ham by coach, and carriage free, as mortal knife had never carved. When Nicholas began to describe Madeline, he sat with his mouth wide open, nudging Mrs. Browdie from time to time, and exclaiming under his breath that she must be "raa'ther a tidy sart," and when he heard at last that his young friend had come down, purposely to communicate his good fortune, and to convey to him all those assurances of friendship which he could not state with sufficient warmth in writing—that the only object of his journey was to share his happiness with them, and to tell them that when he was married they must come up to see him, and that Madeline insisted on it as well as he—John could hold out no longer, but after looking indignantly at his wife, and demanding to know what she was whimpering for, drew his coat-sleeve over his eyes and blubbered outright.

"Tell'ee waa't though," said John seriously, when a great deal had been said on both sides, "to return to schoolmeasther. If this news aboot 'un has reached school to-day, the old 'ooman wean't have a whole boan in her boddy, nor Fanny neither."

"Oh John!" cried Mrs. Browdie.

"Ah! and Oh John agean," replied the Yorkshireman. "I dinnot know what they lads mightn't do. When it first got aboot that schoolmeasther was in trouble, some feythers and moothers sent and took their young chaps awa'. If them as is left, should know waa'ts coom tiv'un, there'll be sike a revolution and rebel!—Ding! But I think they'll a' gang daft, and spill bluid like wather!"

*In fact John Browdie's apprehensions were so strong
that he determined to ride over to the school without delay,
and invited Nicholas to accompany him, which, however, he
declined, pleading that his presence might perhaps
aggravate the bitterness of their adversity.*

*"Thot's true!" said John, "I should ne'er ha' thought o'
thot."*

*"I must return to-morrow," said Nicholas, "but I mean
to dine with you to-day, and if Mrs. Browdie can give me a
bed—"*

*"Bed!" cried John, "I wish thou could'st sleep in fower
beds at once. Ecod thou should'st have 'em a'. Bide till I coom
back; on'y bide till I coom back, and ecod we'll make a day of
it!"*

*Giving his wife a hearty kiss, and Nicholas a no less
hearty shake of the hand, John mounted his horse and rose
off: leaving Mrs. Browdie to apply herself to hospitable
preparations, and his young friend to stroll about the
neighbourhood, and revisit spots which were rendered
familiar to him by many a miserable association.*

*John cantered away, and arriving at Dotheboys hall,
tied his horse to a gate and made his way to the schoolroom
door, which he found locked on the inside. A tremendous
noise and riot arose from within, and, applying his eye to a
convenient crevice in the wall, he did not remain long in
ignorance of its meaning.*

*The news of Squeers's downfall had reached Dotheboys;
that was quite clear. To all appearance, it had very recently
become known to the young gentlemen; for rebellion had just
broken out.*

*It was one of the brimstone and treacle mornings, and
Mrs. Squeers had entered school according to custom with
the large bowl and spoon, followed by Miss Squeers and the
amiable Wackford: who, during his father's absence, had
taken upon himself such minor branches of the executive as
kicking the pupils with his nailed boots, pulling the hair of
some of the smaller boys, pinching the others in aggravating
places, and rendering himself in various similar ways a great
comfort and happiness to his mother. Their entrance,
whether by premeditation or a simultaneous impulse, was
the signal of revolt. While one detachment rushed to the door
and locked it, and another mounted the desks and forms, the
stoutest (and consequently the newest) boy seized the cane,
and confronting Mrs. Squeers, with a stern countenance,
snatched off her cap and beaver bonnet, put it on his own
head, armed himself with the wooden spoon and bade her on
pain of death, go down upn her knees and take a dose
directly. Before that estimable lady could recover herself, or
offer the slightest retaliation, she was forced into a kneeling*

posture by a crowd of shouting tormentors, and compelled to swallow a spoonful of the odious mixture, rendered more than usually savoury by the immersion in the bowl of Master Wackford's head, whose ducking was entrusted to another rebel. The success of this first achievement prompted the ambitious crowd, whose faces were clustered together in every variety of lank and half-starved ugliness, to further acts of outrage. The leader was insisting upon Mrs. Squeers repeating her dose, Master Squeers was undergoing another dip in the treacle, and a violent assault had been commenced on Miss Squeers, when John Browdie, bursting open the door with a vigorous kick, rushed to the rescue. The shouts, screams, groans, hoots, and clapping of hands, suddenly ceased, and a dead silence ensued.

"Ye be noice chaps," said John, looking steadily round. "Waat's to do here, thou yoong dogs?"

"Squeers is in prison, and we are going to run away!" cried a score of shrill voices. "We won't stop, we won't stop!"

"Weel then, dinnot stop," replied John; "who waants thee to stop? Roon awa' loike men, but dinnot hurt the women."

"Hurrah!" cried the shrill voices, more shrilly still.

"Hurrah? repeated John. "Weel, hurrah, loike men too. Noo then, look out. Hip—hip—hip—hurrah!"

"Hurrah!" cried the voices.

"Hurrah! Agean," said John. "Looder still."

The boys obeyed

"Anoother!" said John. "Dinnot be afeared on it. Let's have a good 'un!"

"Hurrah!"

"Noo then," said John, "let's have yan more to end wi', and then coot off as quick as you loike. Tak' a good breath noo—Squeers be in jail—the school's brokken oop—it's a' ower—past and gane— think o' thot, and let it be a hearty 'un! Hurrah!"

Such a cheer arose as the walls of Dotheboys Hall had never echoed before, and were destined never to respond to again. When the sound had died away, the school was empty. and of the busy noisy crowd which had peopled it but five minutes before, not one remained.

"Very well, Mr. Browdie!" said Miss Squeers, hot and flushed from the recent encounter, but vixenish to the last. "you've been and excited out boys to run away. Now see if we don't pay you out for that, sir! If my pa is unfortunate and trod down by henemies, we're not going to be basely crowed and conquered over by you and 'Tilda."

"Noa!" replied John bluntly, "thou bean't Tak' they oath o' thot. Think betther o' us, Fanny. I tell 'ee both, that I'm glod the auld man has been caught out at last—dom'd

*glad—but ye'll sooffer eneaf wi' out any crowin' fra' me, and I
be not the mun to crow, nor be Tilly the lass, so I tell 'ee flat.
More than thot, I tell 'ee noo, that if thou need'st friends to
help thee awa' from this place— dinnot turn up thy nose,
Fanny, thou may'st— thou'lt foind Tilly and I wi' a thout o'
old times aboot us, redy to lend thee a hond. And when I say
thot, dinnot think I be asheamed of waa't I've deane, for I say
ageam, Hurray! And dom the schoolmeasther. There!"*

His parting words concluded, John Browdie strode
heavily out, remounted his nag, put him once more into a
smart canter, and, carolling lustily forth some fragments of
an old song to which the horse's hoofs rang a merry
accompaniment, sped back to his pretty wife and to Nicholas.

For some days afterwards, the neighbouring country
was overrun with boys, who, the report went, had been
secretly furnished by Mr. and Mrs. Browdie, not only with a
hearty meal of bread and meat, but with sundry shillings and
sixpences to help them on their way. To this rumour John
always returned a stout denial, which he accompanied,
however, with a lurking grin, that rendered the suspicious
doubtful, and fully confirmed all previous believers.

There were a few timid young children, who, miserable
as they had been, and many as were the tears they had shed
in the wretched school, still knew no other home, and had
formed for it a sort of attachment which made them weep
when the bolder spirits fled, and cling to it as a refuge. Of
these, some were found crying under hedges and in such
places, frightened by the solitude. One had a dead bird in a
little cage; he had wandered nearly twenty miles, and when
his poor favourite died, lost courage, and lay down beside
him. Another was discovered in a yard hard by the school,
sleeping with a dog, who bit at those who came to remove
him and licked the sleeping child's pale face.

They were taken back, and some other stragglers were
recovered; but by degrees they were claimed, or lost again;
and, in course of time, Dotheboys Hall and its last breaking
up began to be forgotten by the neighbours, or to be only
spoken of, as among the things that had been.'